Jersey 1204

John Le Capelain, 'View across Grouville Bay to
Mont Orgueil Castle', 1812–48 (detail)

J. A. EVERARD & J. C. HOLT

Jersey 1204

The forging of an island community

with 43 illustrations,
28 in colour

Thames & Hudson

The publisher wishes to thank the States of Jersey
and the Jersey Heritage Trust, without whom this
publication would not have been possible.

First published in the United Kingdom in 2004 by
Thames & Hudson Ltd, 181A High Holborn,
London WC1V 7QX

www.thamesandhudson.com

British Library Cataloguing-in-Publication Data
A catalogue record for this book is available from the
British Library

ISBN 0-500-51163-2

Printed and bound in Slovenia by
Mladinska Knjiga Tiskarna

Contents

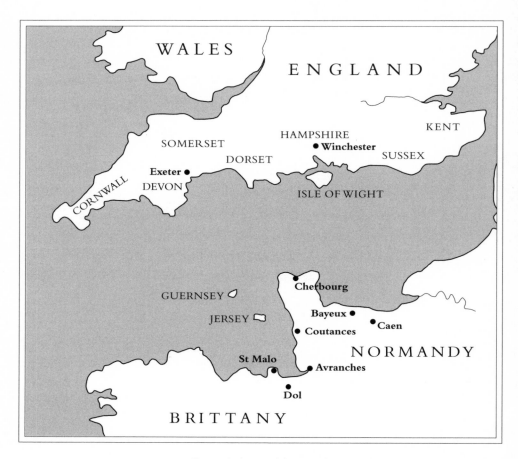

Jersey in its maritime setting

Foreword

BY SIR PHILIP BAILHACHE, BAILIFF OF JERSEY

ARE THE CHANNEL ISLANDS mere rocks around which the tides of European history have insouciantly ebbed and flowed, or have they over the centuries played a significant part in the consideration of those who have ordered the affairs of Europe's nation states? Islanders naturally like to think that their island is the centre of the universe. It is probably true, however, that from the conclusion of the Napoleonic wars until the present time (the period of German Occupation between 1940 and 1945 excepted) the Islands have only rarely surfaced into the general view. This was equally true of the period between the tenth and twelfth centuries when the Norman or Plantagenet empire was at its zenith. Professor John Le Patourel, upon whose work the present authors have placed much reliance, wrote a book entitled *The Norman Empire*, which contains not a single reference to Jersey.

But in 1204, when the unique constitutional status of the Channel Islands was born, it was different. The Islands were part of Normandy and, as the Plantagenet empire began to crumble at the turn of the thirteenth century, they were certainly at the forefront of many minds. They were to remain so intermittently for centuries to come.

The loss of continental Normandy by King John in June 1204 exposed the Islanders to an uncertain future. The Islands were strategically important to the King of England in that they lay conveniently on the sea route to his possessions in Gascony. Furthermore they were a toehold on the edge of Normandy should efforts be made to recover the duchy for the English crown. From the viewpoint of the French king the Islands were

7

part of the territory that he had subdued and were uncomfortably close to his expanded realm. Much later the Islands were described by Victor Hugo (with much poetic licence) as 'morceaux de la France tombés dans la mer et ramassés par l'Angleterre'.

Why then did the Islanders throw in their lot with the English king? They spoke Norman French, they traded with Normandy, their extended families were Norman and ecclesiastically they were bound to the diocese of Coutances. The authors have provided some carefully researched and novel answers to this perennial question. They describe the macro-political forces deriving from the ownership of land in Normandy and England, the tenurial revolution resulting from the removal of Norman seigneurs from the local scene, and the influence of powerful courtiers holding office under the Crown. They do not ignore the micro-political forces deriving from the decisions to establish a separate administration, to decree the continuance in force of Norman and local customary laws, and to preserve established religious ties with the see of Coutances, all of which no doubt contributed to the maintenance of local support and goodwill.

The emergence of this valuable study, commissioned by the States of Jersey as part of the celebrations of the 800th anniversary of 1204, is greatly to be welcomed. The scholarly approach to the genesis of Jersey as a quasi-autonomous small nation state is a worthy addition to the bibliography of the island's constitutional history. The character and resilience of an island people are forged by the past. This book will provide food for much stimulating conversation and debate as the Bailiwick and its people rejoice in their heritage and assert their national identity at the beginning of a new chapter in their history.

Preface

COLLABORATIVE WORK gives rise to memories – Monypenny and Buckle, Pollock and Maitland, and so on. I cannot now recall what Monypenny did for Buckle or Buckle for Monypenny in their six ponderous volumes on the life of Benjamin Disraeli. The case of Pollock and Maitland's *History of English Law* is clear enough: Sir Frederick Pollock wrote the chapter on Anglo-Saxon law and Maitland (to our great benefit) wrote the rest.

No such sharp chronological division could be made in the present book. However, some further prefatory remarks of Pollock fit exactly:

> It is proper for me to add for myself that, although the book was planned in common and has been revised by both of us, by far the greater share of the execution belongs to Mr Maitland, both as to the actual writing and as to the detailed research which was constantly required.

So this is Dr Everard's book just as Pollock and Maitland was Maitland's. I decided very early that it was quite impossible to mingle two styles; the result would have been a patchwork quilt. Nevertheless, our approaches were identical, the result of long association and prolonged discussion. I have read the work throughout and made suggestions. Here and there I have recommended the addition of a paragraph or two to introduce new themes, but not often and not many. The reader will be challenged to determine where I have stepped in.

It is a pleasure to record the overriding interest of John Mills, the day-to-day attention of Michael Day and of his ever watchful secretary, Stephanie Skudder. Mr Douglas Ford was meticulous in chasing our requirements for illustrations and also provided some of his own. We benefited from the hospitality of the Société Jersiaise where the Executive Secretary, Mrs Pauline Syvret, was always welcoming and helpful. In the Library Mrs Angela Underwood and Mrs Anna Baghiani sustained our enquiries with ready efficiency. To all these we extend our thanks.

Nearer home Dr Helen Evans gave us generous guidance in the early stages of our researches. Later Mrs Olive Everard read a complete draft of the book and Mr Nicholas Syms gave his close attention to the first chapter. Finally, like all scholars in Cambridge, we are deeply in debt to the University Library and its staff.

James Holt
Fitzwilliam College, Cambridge
1 January 2004

Introduction

LIKE MOST SMALL ISLANDS Jersey was vulnerable – vulnerable to invasion and settlement, vulnerable to external control, vulnerable to influences flowing in from all kinds of sources over which the islanders had little sway. So it was in 1204. Jersey was part of the duchy of Normandy, the homeland and origin of the Norman kings of England, but in 1204 the English lost the duchy to the French. Château Gaillard, the great fortress that Richard Lionheart had built above Les Andelys, on the narrows of the River Seine, fell on 6 March 1204. Thereafter Philip of France marched through central and western Normandy: castle after castle and town after town surrendered. Then Philip returned east to accept the surrender of Rouen on 24 June, and by the end of the year the French reconquest was complete. 'Reconquest'? So it seemed and seems to the French; English historians have taken a different view, traditionally referring to 'the loss of Normandy' as though the duchy were part of an empire, now lost if not for ever at least for a good many years to come.

What did the men of Jersey (and the other Channel Islands) make of it, as they exchanged news and gossip in their church-yards after service? They were ill prepared and must have been astonished at the rapid collapse of the old Normandy. They had become accustomed to the rule of the successors to the Norman kings, the Plantagenets, who, if they had imposed more disci-plined and sophisticated forms of government, had also widened the horizons of the Channel Islanders and secured their trade and traffic throughout the Western English Channel as far as the borders of Spain. So what was to be done now? The links with the see of Coutances were at risk, and Coutances had long been the mother church of the Islanders. Where were those landed families who held estates both in Jersey and in western Normandy to turn with their allegiance? And perhaps above all else, what was to be the source of legitimate government now that Caen, the site of the Norman Exchequer, had submitted to the King of France?

The problems facing Jersey were immediate and local. But their source was not local. It sprang rather from the vast extent and complexity of the dominions of the Plantagenet kings. In 1202 these had begun to implode: Brittany first, then Anjou, then unrest among the lords on the border of Anjou and southern Normandy, then the treason (as King John called it) of Robert, Count of Séez, which involved the surrender of Alençon and the eradication of Plantagenet authority from the whole of southern Normandy, thus destroying their control of the lines of communication south to Le Mans and Angers. In the Channel Islands these disasters were no more than the distant drums of war. They were soon to be at hand.

After the invasion of Normandy in 1204, the people of Jersey were faced with the stark choice of following their compatriots on the mainland in the French allegiance, or continuing to support King John. That they chose for the Plantagenets is well-known. Indeed there is a constant reminder of this choice in the society of modern Jersey and its constitutional status as a peculiar of the Crown of England. The question that has hitherto defied satisfactory answer is, 'Why?' What made the people of Jersey so different from their friends and neighbours on the nearby mainland that they should choose the opposite, hostile, political allegiance? This divergence was by no means inevitable, in fact the French succeeded in invading Jersey twice, first in 1204 and again in 1216.

Previous studies of Jersey in the aftermath of 1204 have concentrated on the institutions of the Plantagenet administration and the role of the Crown, issuing mandates from England and Gascony. While royal government is an important part of the story, we have also tried to take account of the story of those men (and women) of Jersey, gossiping in their parish churchyards. It is they, we believe, who hold the key to the origins of modern Jersey.

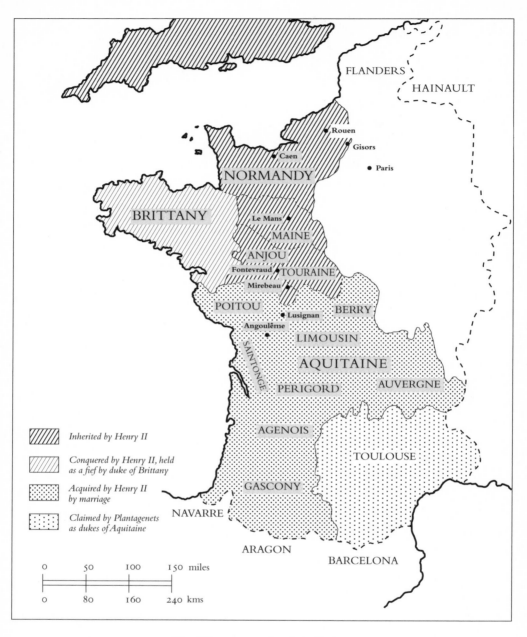

The Plantagenet lands in France, *c.* 1200

CHAPTER ONE

The Plantagenet empire and the loss of Normandy

IN 1200, King John ruled over one of the greatest empires in the history of medieval Christendom. King of England, he claimed sovereignty over Ireland and demanded loyalty and obedience from the king of the Scots and the princes of Wales. On the Continent, John was Duke of Normandy, Duke of Aquitaine and Count of Anjou, and received the homage of the Duke of Brittany. The Channel Islands, too, were securely tucked under the Plantagenet mantle, as an integral part of the duchy of Normandy. In effect, the territory of most of the British Isles and the western half of modern France was under Plantagenet sovereignty. So great and far-flung were the dominions under Plantagenet rule that 'empire' is the only modern term that seems apt to describe them. The Plantagenet empire was not ancient; it was the work of John's father, Henry II. But having passed intact from Henry to his eldest surviving son, Richard I 'the Lionheart', and thence to his younger son, John, the arrangement was beginning to take on an air of permanency. The customary laws of western France (and England) were in their favour in that they distinguished between acquisition and inheritance, giving vastly greater weight to the latter; it amounted to title.

Plantagenet rule on the Continent was not unchallenged, however. Apart from rebellious barons, the threat came from the king of France. By 1200, the Capetian 'kings of Francia' had not exercised any real control over the western and southern parts of their realm for over two hundred years. Nevertheless, their sovereignty over these regions was sanctified by long tradition dating from the reign of the Emperor Charlemagne and beyond. In 1204, the king of France struck. Philip II invaded the duchy of Normandy, and in July 1214 his victory at the battle of Bouvines ended Plantagenet rule in France north of the Loire. For his achievements in extending the territories under French royal power, Philip II was acclaimed 'Augustus' by his classically-educated biographer. By June 1204, the whole of the duchy of Normandy was in the control of the French king. The conse-quences of 1204 for the Channel Islands cannot be understood without taking into account the broader perspective of the struggle between the Plantagenet kings of England and the Capetian kings of France for sovereignty over the western half of France.

How did the kings of England come to make such extravagant claims over French soil? In the first place, the kings of England from 1066 to 1204 would not have identified themselves as 'English'. Rather they were great French magnates – dukes of Normandy, and, from the mid-twelfth century, also dukes of Aquitaine and counts of Anjou. 'Anjou' at this time meant the combined counties of Anjou, Maine and the Touraine, in fact the entire middle and lower Loire valley and its hinterland. Henry II was born at Le Mans, and his anguish at seeing that city in flames in 1189 hastened his death. He could not speak the English ver-nacular, although he did visit England often and for extended periods from boyhood. Richard I was born in England but visited infrequently after his investiture as count of Poitou in 1172, and notoriously spent only six months in England during his ten-year reign as king. John was also born in England, but as a young boy he was sent to the abbey of Fontevraud to be educated as a French aristocrat, and later chose a bride from Aquitaine. The heartland of the first Plantagenet kings was the Loire valley, an attachment reflected in their choice of the abbey of Fontevraud as their final resting place.

The crown of England, won by Duke William II of Normandy, 'the Conqueror', and fought over by his descendants for the next hundred years, was but one more title or 'honour' to this dynasty. Nevertheless, the importance of the kingship should not be underestimated, since it brought advantages both financial and ideological. England was a fertile, prosperous country. The centralized government developed by the later Anglo-Saxon kings meant that the country's wealth was efficiently exploited for the benefit of the royal treasury. In addition, a matter perhaps of equal importance was the unique prestige of kingship. Once crowned and anointed, the king of England was the social and spiritual equal of the king of France. He was no longer just one of the various magnates of France who rivalled the king in material wealth and power.

At the same time, the kings of France, the lineal descendants of Hugh Capet (987–96), were far from being masters of their own kingdom. By 1150, the Capetian king Louis VII could only exercise any effective authority in the region around Paris, the Ile-de-France, between the Seine and Loire. This was in fact an improvement on the situation a generation earlier. In the reign of Louis VI, it was said, travellers needed an armed guard to travel the road between Paris and Orléans. Such was the rapacity of the local castellans, amongst whom royal authority was respected more in the breach than the observance. Surrounding the Ile-de-France were the numerous duchies, counties and viscounties, the 'territorial principalities', whose rulers had escaped royal authority since the breakdown of the regime of the Carolingian kings, and which were now effectively autonomous. It was in these circumstances that Normandy, Aquitaine, Brittany, Anjou, Maine and the Touraine could become united in the hands of one great magnate dynasty, the Plantagenets.

The only thing that saved the Capetian king from being just one among many great magnates ruling his own petty principality was the ideology of kingship. In the institution of monarchy was embodied the memory that there had once been a kingdom of 'West Francia' (later just 'Francia'), the western portion of Charlemagne's empire, a realm of nearly the same extent as modern France. This memory was assiduously cultivated in the writings of the sophisticated intellectuals of the Capetian court, such as Suger, abbot of the royal abbey of Saint-Denis. Documents issued in the king's name by the scribes of the royal chancery were embellished with high-flown rhetoric about the king's sovereignty over the whole kingdom, in stark contrast to the actual scope of royal government. The propaganda worked: the prestige of the Capetian kings was never diminished. By the mid-twelfth century the Capetian kings were following the trend set by some of the magnates, not least the Plantagenets. They increased the range of their authority into all corners of their 'principalities', the Ile-de-France in the case of the Capetians, and at the same time made their authority more effective through innovations in government and administration.

This development, however, made increasingly imminent what had always been a potential for conflict between the king and the magnates. Before the thirteenth century, the magnates were not under any obligation to render homage to the king. Even if they did render homage, it was as an act of friendship and alliance. The 'law of fiefs' had not yet been developed to the stage where homage meant that the vassal held his lands of the lord (in this case, the king) in return for performing specific services, and that the lord had the right to deprive him of those lands if he should default on those obligations. But the thinking at the French king's court was heading that way, as King John would find to his cost in 1202. In the eleventh and twelfth centuries, it was still possible for a magnate to render homage to the king without substantially undermining his own authority. The purpose of such an act of homage was to give legitimacy to the magnate's own claims to authority over his land and people against challenges from others. The dukes of Normandy maintained a policy of rendering homage only at the frontier, usually at or near Gisors. In order to demonstrate their autonomy they refused to travel outside Normandy at the king's summons.

The counts of Anjou were historically closer to the Capetian regime. The Norman dukes originated as Viking settlers who had arrived in the area formerly known as Neustria and carved a place for themselves at Rouen, independently of the enfeebled monarchy. In contrast, the ancestors of the counts of Anjou were officials employed by the Carolingian and then the early Capetian administrations in the Loire valley. In spite of their extraordinary rise to power to become rivals to the kings they had once served, this relationship was remembered and even cultivated. Early in the reign of Henry II, it was still plausible to invoke a tradition that the hereditary office of steward of the Capetian royal household, or 'Seneschal of France', belonged to the count of Anjou, and hence to Henry II personally. According to the chronicler Gervase of Canterbury, when Henry II invaded southern Brittany in 1158, he did so as 'Seneschal of France' and with the assent of Louis VII, although Henry II's invasion of Brittany was entirely self-serving. When Philip Augustus made Henry II's son, Geoffrey of Brittany, 'Seneschal of France' in 1185, it was tantamount to recognizing Geoffrey as Count of Anjou. So it was acceptable for a great magnate, even the king of England, to acknowledge himself a subordinate of the Capetian king when it suited his own ends.

In the eleventh and twelfth centuries, magnates could render homage to the king at times when it was politically expedient for them to do so, because the consequences did not impinge greatly on their political autonomy. Even if the obligations upon the vassal had been more onerous, the Capetians would not have been able to enforce them against the Plantagenets. Hence the anomalous situation arose that the king of England was the vassal of the king of France for his Continental possessions. This was to become increasingly untenable as the authority exercised by both kings over their lands and their peoples grew.

The Anglo-Norman realm created in 1066 lasted for nearly a hundred and fifty years. In contrast, the 'Plantagenet empire' in its fullest extent was a relatively brief phenomenon, lasting only from 1154 to 1204. It began with the succession of Henry, eldest son of Geoffrey Plantagenet, Count of Anjou. Geoffrey had conquered Normandy, claiming it as the inheritance of his wife, the Empress Matilda, daughter of Henry I, King of England and Duke of Normandy. In 1152, their son, the young Duke Henry married Eleanor, heiress of the duchy of Aquitaine. Combining the ambitious territorial claims of the three houses of Normandy, Anjou and Aquitaine, Henry now asserted lordship over territories comprising approximately the western half of modern France. Even then, it was not at all certain that Henry would succeed in making good his mother's claim to the throne of England. The Plantagenet cause was flagging there and King Stephen was preparing to crown his son Eustace to ensure his succession. It was only the premature death of Eustace that smoothed the way for negotiations and the acceptance of Henry as Stephen's heir. Henry II's coronation at Westminster in December 1154 completed the 'Plantagenet empire'. Further campaigns in Wales and Ireland did not add materially to Henry II's wealth but did neutralize potential political dissensions and extend his political authority. The duchy of Brittany was conquered between 1158 and 1168, to be ruled directly by Henry II until 1181 and thereafter by one of his younger sons, Geoffrey, and his heirs.

It is quite possible that Henry II did not expect his vast conglomeration of territories to last for longer than his own lifetime. In 1169 he made it known that he intended to divide his lands between his three sons, Henry, Richard and Geoffrey. John, the youngest, was a mere infant and was not taken into account; hence he was known as John 'Lackland'. Whatever the king's personal wishes or political judgment, the division was strictly in accordance with the succession practices of the French aristocracy of the day, which distinguished between land a man obtained by inheritance (the patrimony) and lands acquired by marriage or other means. The patrimony should pass, undivided, to the eldest son; the remainder might be used to provide for daughters and younger sons. If one son received the patrimony and also lands acquired by his father, then, in the son's hands, all became 'patrimony' to be passed undivided to *his* eldest son. In the case of the Plantagenets, Henry the Young King, the eldest son, was to inherit the patrimony, the lands Henry II had inherited from his own mother and father, that is, the kingdom of England, the duchy of Normandy and the county of Anjou. The next son, Richard, was to inherit the land Henry II had acquired by marriage, that is, the duchy of Aquitaine. Another younger son, Geoffrey, was to inherit the land acquired by conquest, that is, the duchy of Brittany. Following the same principle, John was later made 'lord of Ireland', another of Henry II's conquests, albeit a very incomplete one.

By the reign of Henry II, no one would have envisaged the separation of England and Normandy. The kingdom and the duchy had formed the patrimony of the Anglo-Norman royal family since the death of William the Conqueror and were to remain united in the hands of the senior branch of the family. Their tenure was sanctioned by time and custom. The 'Anglo-Norman realm' was already venerable and, even without the authority of succession custom, there was no reason for it to be divided. Even though England and Normandy were administered separately, there were factors that encouraged unity, such as similar institutions of government and an aristocracy possessing land on both sides of the Channel. There was also the pressure of history: England and Normandy were the legacy of Henry's grandfather, Henry I, and one of Henry II's guiding principles was to restore and enjoy for himself the authority his grandfather had exercised.

Beyond the Anglo-Norman realm, Henry II intended his lands to be divided between his sons and their descendants after him. It was by a remote chance that the patrimony in fact survived intact into the next generation. Henry the Young King and then Richard died, in turn, without legitimate issue. Geoffrey also died young, before Richard, leaving a posthumous son, Arthur of Brittany. On the death of King Richard I in April 1199, John 'Lackland' inherited from his elder brother, as patrimony, the Angevin, or Plantagenet, 'empire' complete – England, Wales and Ireland, Normandy, Greater Anjou, Aquitaine and Brittany. Acquisition had become inheritance.

'Empire' may be the most apt term for this conglomeration of territories, but it is not a perfect fit. Some historians feel quite uncomfortable about using it, and will only do so if it is safely constrained by quotation marks. Historians of the nineteenth and early twentieth century were almost inevitably drawn to perceive the Plantagenet empire as a precursor to the British empire of their own day – English historians with pride (and disappointment at its demise), French historians with a certain antipathy. In more recent decades, a reaction has set in and the 'imperial' character of the Plantagenet regime has been questioned and found wanting. It was mere dynastic and political good fortune that Henry II was able to accumulate so many territories under his own dominion, there was no logical reason for them to remain united after his death, and there were no institutions that gave this conglomeration of territories any coherence. There is furthermore no evidence that in the twelfth century anyone regarded Henry II as an 'emperor'. The only emperor there could be in Western Christendom was the ruler of the Holy Roman Empire, the political successor of the emperors of ancient Rome. The word 'imperium', occasionally used by contemporaries to describe the Plantagenet regime, meant simply 'power'. Nevertheless, 'Plantagenet empire' remains the most useful expression, with these caveats in mind.

One of the chief flaws in the 'empire' analogy lies in the way the Plantagenet empire was governed. A narrow interpretation of the term 'empire' requires there to be at least some centralization and coordination of institutions. In the Plantagenet empire, the only element of centralization was the king's person. The king was permanently on the move, travelling around his vast dominions, radiating royal authority and offering royal patronage in the immediate locality wherever he went. Wherever the king was, he would make decisions which could apply to any part of his dominions, or to all of them. Most decisions were *ad hoc* and dealt with particular cases. Parties to a legal dispute in England who needed the king's writ to proceed with litigation had to follow the king, all the way to the south of France if necessary, to obtain it. Royal acts which we would recognize as legislative and which were intended to apply uniformly to a whole province, or more than one of them, were very few, but the fact that any were made at all demonstrates the possibility of the development of some uniformity throughout the 'empire'.

The absence of centralized institutions was not a matter of default, but a deliberate policy. Count Geoffrey Plantagenet had counselled his son Henry to govern each of his different domin- ions according to its own customs, and this is what Henry and his sons did. Each separate territory, each duchy or even county, under Plantagenet rule was governed separately from the others. The Plantagenet ruler exercised authority in Anjou not in the capacity of 'emperor' or king of England, but as the count of Anjou. He had just as many, or as few, rights and obligations in respect of the people and the territory of Anjou as had his predecessors as counts. The same was true of the Plantagenets' ducal authority in Normandy and Aquitaine. These different territorial principalities had much in common in the way of institutions of government, as they did in culture, language and religion, but these similarities were born of their shared heritage as parts of the former Frankish empire of Charlemagne, not by any uniformity imposed by the Plantagenets.

In the past, each duke or count had resided in his own territory, itinerating around that limited area, between castles, abbeys and palaces, exercising his ducal or comital authority in person. Each castle or other estate that was exploited directly for the lord's benefit (rather than being held as fiefs by the military aristocracy or in alms by the church) had its resident officials to collect rents and 'customary' dues, and to administer justice in minor matters. These came under a variety of titles: 'senescallus' (steward or seneschal), 'vicecomes' (*vicomte*), 'prepositus' (*prévôt*), 'vicarius', or the generic terms 'minister' or 'ballivus'. When the duke or count visited, these officials accounted to him for the conduct of their duties, and for the sums they had collected and disbursed.

In England and Normandy, at least, the typical arrangement whereby the local official was remunerated, and motivated, was that rather than rendering all the payments he collected, and then receiving a salary, he held his post at farm. This meant that the approximate value of the particular office, in terms of its annual revenues to the king/duke, was assessed. This was represented as a lump sum, the 'firma', which the official was then obliged to pay to the treasury each year. Any surplus collected represented the official's remuneration. But each year there were extraordinary items of expenditure incurred or revenues not collected which the official wished to have taken into account and deducted from his 'farm'. This occurred, for example, when the king/duke rewarded a third party with a portion of the revenues, or with exemption from paying a debt.

More important judicial cases were also determined personally by the duke or count sitting in his court, aided by his faithful barons and churchmen. Clearly, this degree of personal involvement in government was not possible when one individual had so many provinces to govern. This problem had already arisen in England and Normandy after 1066, and institutions had evolved in the kingdom and the duchy to address it. Essentially, the solution was to create a viceregal office: one individual would be the king/duke/count's deputy, authorized to exercise full royal, ducal or comital powers in the ruler's absence. In England, this was the Chief Justiciar. In Normandy, and in each of the other Continental territories, the same powers were delegated to the Seneschal. The old estate officials continued as before, now answerable to the seneschal, but also directly answerable to the Plantagenet ruler if he happened to address them in a written mandate or pay a visit to the region. The seneschal was aided by other officials with responsibility for the whole of the duchy or county, including a constable ('constabularius') for military matters. Royal/ducal/comital jurisdiction was also exercised by judges ('justicii' or 'justiciarii') specially commissioned to sit, as appropriate, either at a particular location or on circuit. The individuals to whom these important offices were entrusted were almost without exception natives of the provinces in which they acted. One would not normally find a Poitevin as Seneschal of Normandy, or a Norman as Seneschal of Anjou. Similarly, the custom developed of having the royal officials render their financial accounts, as described above, at special sessions of the king/duke's court, without the ruler himself necessarily being present. This session was known as the Exchequer, and separate Exchequers were held for royal revenues in England at Westminster and for ducal revenues in Normandy at Caen (plate 6).

This history of institutions is important in providing an explanation for the rapid fragmentation and demise of the Plantagenet empire. Once the king's person was removed there was nothing to bind the different provinces together into any sort of political unit. The royal officials themselves were primarily interested in the welfare of the regions under their control, where their family estates and all their financial and emotional interests lay. It was in this respect simple and almost painless to transfer whole provinces from Plantagenet sovereignty to Capetian. In Normandy, for instance, the hereditary constable, William du Hommet, and his extended family were among the first to transfer their allegiance to Philip Augustus.

One area where there was an element of uniformity across the Plantagenet empire was in coinage. In keeping with their virtual autonomy from the kings of France, from the eleventh century the various dukes and counts minted their own coins. In the straitened economic circumstances of western Europe after the collapse of the Carolingian empire, the only coins minted were silver denarii, although sums of money were reckoned in pounds, shillings and pence, or libri (*livres*), solidi (*sous*) and denarii (*deniers*). While these mostly circulated only in the region where they were minted, some had a remarkably wide circulation, such as the debased coins minted at Guingamp in northern Brittany. English pennies 'sterling' were especially valuable: the close royal control of minting and high silver content made them worth four times as much as some of the so-called 'feudal' coins of France. Before 1154, the other principal coinage circulating in the Anglo-Norman realm was the *denier* of Rouen, the ducal mint of Normandy. After 1154, Henry II suppressed the Rouen mint and promoted instead the *deniers* of Angers, the coinage minted by the counts of Anjou. *Deniers angevins* became a sort of official currency for the Plantagenets' Continental possessions north of the Loire until 1204. Pennies sterling and *deniers* of Guingamp, Le Mans and other 'feudal' mints continued to be current, but were subject to a fixed rate of exchange. One penny sterling was worth two *deniers* of Le Mans and four *deniers* minted elsewhere in the Plantagenet empire. This had the great advantage that payments rendered in a variety of different *deniers* could be reckoned with certainty.

The existence of a co-ordinated, if not uniform, currency between England and western France, along with Plantagenet control of the seaways of the English Channel and the Atlantic coast of France, demonstrates that, 'empire' aside, the Plantagenets did preside over a vast commercial trading zone. One of Henry II's first acts after taking control of the county of Nantes, at the mouth of the Loire, in 1158 was to order a consignment of wine to be shipped from there to England. This trading zone was greatly to the benefit of all who lived within it, and not least the Channel Islanders.

Only five years after John's succession, and fifty years after its inception, the 'Plantagenet empire' was eviscerated by the loss of Normandy to Philip Augustus. The 'empire' did not, however, disappear and cease to exist. For a few more years the Plantagenets clung to parts of Anjou and Poitou. After 1224, the remaining 'Plantagenet empire' consisted, rather improbably, of its two most far-flung members, the British Isles (where Plantagenet authority over Wales and Ireland was progressively increased) and Gascony, the southern portion of the former duchy of Aquitaine. These were linked by the one other remaining Plantagenet possession, the Channel Islands.

The loss of Normandy was a severe blow to King John and the Anglo-Norman aristocracy. Like Henry II and Richard I before him, John had been girded with the ceremonial sword of the dukes of Normandy before he crossed to England to be crowned king.

denier angevin, twelfth century

The *denier* of Anjou would have been the common currency in Jersey from the mid-twelfth century until 1204. Coins from other mints in the Plantagenet dominions were also legal tender, including English pennies sterling. A penny of the type illustrated here, dating from *c.* 1185, was recently found where it had been dropped on the floor of a house in St Helier. After 1204, Philip Augustus introduced the *denier tournois* to replace the *denier angevin* in the former Plantagenet territories north of the Loire. The *denier angevin* and the *denier tournois* were equivalent to each other in value; both were worth only one-quarter of a penny sterling.

short-cross penny of Henry II

denier tournois of Philip Augustus

It is no coincidence that the Capetian kings of France from 1204 insisted on keeping Normandy in their own hands, whereas other recent acquisitions, including the counties of Anjou and Poitou, were given to younger sons and grandsons of Philip Augustus. Normandy was too great a prize, and too great a temptation to the Plantagenets, to be entrusted to any individual as 'duke of Normandy'. The loss of Normandy is also the most relevant chapter in the demise of the 'Plantagenet empire' from our point of view, because the Channel Islands were part of Normandy, and hence the Islands also were 'lost' to the English crown in 1204.

Such a dramatic turn of fortune, between 1199 and 1204, could not have been the result of a single event or cause. Rather, a number of factors combined in 1204 to enable Philip Augustus to conquer Normandy with little resistance. The comparative strengths of the Plantagenet and Capetian monarchies are the first consideration. Comparing the vast and wealthy dominions of the Plantagenets with the Capetians' Ile-de-France suggests a very unequal competition, one that King John could only have lost by rank incompetence and mismanagement. For a long time, the loss of Normandy was indeed blamed on John's personal failings. However, on closer inspection, the inequality was not so great as appears at first glance. While England and Normandy were highly organized and centralized states by twelfth-century standards, the nature and degree of Plantagenet authority elsewhere on the Continent much more closely resembled that of the Capetians in the lands under their control. That is, the authority of the count of Anjou and the duke of Aquitaine was mediated through the provincial aristocracy and the ecclesiastical hierarchy. Not all of the areas marked pink on some old maps of France were ruled in the same way. In the south-east, some represented mere long-standing territorial claims by the dukes of Aquitaine, which the Plantagenets, notably Richard I, invested huge efforts in vainly trying to make good.

The kingdom of England was renowned for its wealth, which could be efficiently and at times rapaciously exploited by the Plantagenet kings, but converting the wealth of the royal treasury in England into fighting men in France was expensive and fraught with risk, not least of shipwreck. During the 1190s, the English economy was exploited as never before by Richard I, first to finance his crusade and then to pay his ransom, and on top of that to finance his endless military campaigns in France. King John has been criticized for levying extortionate taxes on the people of England to finance his military expeditions, but he was doing no more than following Richard's example. John suffered from the fact that, by the time he was crowned, the financial demands and depredations had been going on for ten years; the coffers were running low and popular resentment running high before John's reign even started. So England was not the endless source of ready cash the Plantagenet kings had come to expect; in fact it was in danger of being bled dry.

Meanwhile, since 1154 the Capetian kings Louis VII and his son Philip Augustus had been quietly increasing their authority, both in quantity and quality. Before the late twelfth century, the French monarchy was notoriously hard-up. Louis VII, by nature ascetic, is reported to have said 'merrily' to an English visitor to his court, '...your lord, the king of England, who wants for nothing, has men, horses, gold, silk, jewels, fruits, game, and everything else. We in France have nothing but bread, wine and gaiety.'[1] Perhaps the Capetians were luring their rivals into a false sense of security. They had been steadily improving the administration of the Ile-de-France to the extent that it rivalled that of Anjou, if not Normandy. The Ile-de-France had also singularly benefited from the great economic expansion of the twelfth century. Its climate, topography and situation at the meeting of important north-south trade routes with major rivers encouraged agricultural production, commercial activity and a consequent increase in

31

population. All this increased the king's revenue from taxation and his military resources. In addition, the astute marriage of Philip Augustus to Isabella of Hainault, the niece of the Count of Flanders, brought the Crown valuable possessions in the Low Countries. The lands of the counts of Flanders were in advance even of Normandy in terms of both administrative efficiency and urbanization, and Philip Augustus acquired a share of this lucrative region. It also gave the land-locked Ile-de-France access to the North Sea, and hence to England. The 1190s has been termed 'the decisive decade' for the Capetian monarchy, the period in which it increased in wealth and military capability to rival the Plantagenets on the French mainland.

Philip Augustus had the additional advantage that in any conflict with the Plantagenets at the frontiers of Normandy and Anjou, he could muster his military forces by land over relatively short distances. They would not expend too much effort in arriving at the theatre of battle, nor too much time, an important consideration when the knights only owed military service at their own expense for a certain period, normally forty days. The enormous extent of the Plantagenet dominions was a positive disadvantage here, especially in the difficulties of bringing military forces from England by sea. Even if the total military resources available to Philip Augustus in 1204 were fewer than those available to John, the Capetian king could use what he had more efficiently and economically.

The study of 'great men' in history may no longer be fashionable, but there is something to be said for comparing and contrasting the rival kings in this instance. King Louis VII, a careful and thoughtful man, had known he could not overthrow Henry II, but had worked assiduously to undermine him by diplomatic means whenever the opportunity arose. He had supported King Stephen and his son Eustace in their conflict with the Plantagenets in Normandy, he gave shelter to Thomas Becket during his exile, and later encouraged Henry the Young King (married to Louis' own daughter) to rebel against Henry II in 1173. Philip Augustus was as intelligent and careful as his father, but less hindered by moral scruples. He learned the same technique of dividing the Plantagenet family, but was able to deploy it finally with devastating effect because of more favourable circumstances.

The favourable circumstances were that John's succession in 1199 was not unchallenged. His nephew, Arthur of Brittany, had a claim to be the heir of Richard I which was as good as, if not better than, John's. At thirteen, Arthur was nearly an adult by twelfth-century standards, and on learning of Richard's death he immediately marched on the Angevin heartland and was invested as Count of Anjou. Philip Augustus leapt at the chance to encourage dissension and division, and offered his support to Arthur in the ensuing military conflict. Rather than genuine sympathy with Arthur's cause, this was probably a strategy devised to gain an advantage over John. When the kings made peace in 1200, John was forced to pay the price for Philip withdrawing his support for Arthur by rendering homage for all his French lands, which John acknowledged he and his heirs would henceforth hold of the French crown.

Two years later, Philip duly exercised his rights as 'seigneur' and ordered the confiscation of these same lands on the grounds that John had defaulted in his obligations as vassal. Again, this was Philip masterfully seizing an opportunity to undermine the Plantagenet's authority without resorting to military force. The story has been told many times. For reasons which have never been adequately explained, John divorced his Anglo-Norman wife, Isabella, heiress of the earldom of Gloucester, and married instead another Isabella, heiress of the county of Angoulême in Aquitaine. Isabella was inconveniently already betrothed to the young son of Hugh IX de Lusignan, who did not consent to the arrangement being broken off. The Lusignan family appealed to the King of France to bring John, the King's vassal and their lord as Duke of Aquitaine, to justice.

In April 1202 Philip Augustus summoned John to appear at the French royal court in Paris. John refused: as an anointed king, how could he obey the summons of another? Philip judged that John's lands were forfeit for his disobedience to the summons. Armed with his own legal judgment as justification, Philip attempted to seize the duchy of Normandy and offered all of John's other Continental territories to Arthur, now Duke of Brittany, to hold of the French crown. Soon afterwards, while campaigning in Poitou, John captured Arthur, his sister Eleanor and many of their supporters. Arthur disappeared, and is presumed to have died while in captivity in Normandy in the spring of 1203. Philip Augustus maintained the offensive, now with the support of the Bretons, antagonized by the murder of their young duke. The Capetian advance was checked at Château Gaillard, the great fortress on the Seine built by Richard I (plate 4). In December 1203, John left Normandy for the last time. If he had seriously hoped to muster reinforcements in England in time to save the rest of the duchy, those hopes were dashed with the fall of Château Gaillard on 6 March 1204. Philip Augustus followed this military success with careful strategy. Instead of marching straight for Rouen, which was expected to withstand a long siege, the Capetian king diverted his army to invade the heart of Normandy. Resistance here would be less concentrated, and if the plan succeeded, the defenders of Rouen would have less hope of relief and less reason to defend the city. The Capetians took Argentan and Falaise, meeting little resistance from the Normans along the way. The Bretons, under their duke-regent, Guy de Thouars, simultaneously crossed the western frontier, took Avranches and met Philip Augustus at Caen. From there Philip Augustus took a more direct route to Rouen, which duly surrendered on 24 June 1204. With the fall of Rouen, all of Normandy was lost to the Plantagenets.

Even if the relative positions of the two kings were comparable by 1204, it still remains to be explained why the inhabitants of Normandy did not resist the Capetian invasion with any great vehemence. Since the Channel Islanders were also Normans, this question applies to them too. One possibility is that the Normans no longer considered the Plantagenet king to be their natural lord. The kings themselves were keen to be invested as dukes of Normandy in order to exploit the duchy's wealth, but what did the Normans receive in return? They no longer enjoyed the duke's presence, a source of justice and bounty, in their midst. Since 1154, the duke of Normandy had also been the ruler of vast and far-flung dominions which could only be ruled by continuous itineration. Compared with the Norman dukes of old, even compared with Henry I, Henry II and his sons were often absent from the duchy.

It seems that King John did nothing to win back the affections of the Normans. In divorcing his Anglo-Norman bride and marrying Isabella of Angoulême, he showed favour for Isabella's Poitevin kin and countrymen with royal patronage. He left Normandy at the end of 1203 and declined to return to give his personal support to the defenders. In fact, John's employment of large numbers of mercenary soldiers for the defence of Normandy was a particular cause of grievance, as the foreign mercenaries plundered and ravaged the communities they were supposed to be protecting. This must have been all the more infuriating to the Normans, given that the onerous financial exactions demanded of them by the ducal state were largely being used to finance the war.

Furthermore, as the rendering of homage to the king of France became a more regular occurrence and acquired more legal significance under Philip Augustus, the idea became current that the Capetian king was the sovereign of all of France and the superior lord of Normandy; even the duke now acknowledged it. In these circumstances, the Capetian king was hardly a foreign power, to be feared and resisted. Rather, as sovereign or as feudal lord, he was entitled to take the duchy into his own hands in appropriate circumstances. By cutting out the 'middle man', the tenants-in-chief of the duke of Normandy – those who held their land directly of the duke – would become, at a stroke, tenants-in-chief of the king of France. Indeed, in a sense this was all that happened. The sovereignty of Normandy did not change from King John to Philip Augustus, because the king of France was the sovereign before 1204. Rather, one stage in the 'feudal hierarchy', the duke, was simply removed.

So the duchy of Normandy was irrevocably lost to the Plantagenets. With the wisdom of hindsight, this seems a perfectly natural and reasonable development. Obviously the king of France should rule all of his own kingdom, and just as obviously the king of England could not sustain a claim to rule over part of France. But this simple certainty is confounded when we consider the Channel Islands, lost to the Plantagenets in 1204 but thereafter reconquered. The rest of this book will focus on the history of the Islands, specifically Jersey, and attempt to explain their extraordinary relationship with the English crown.

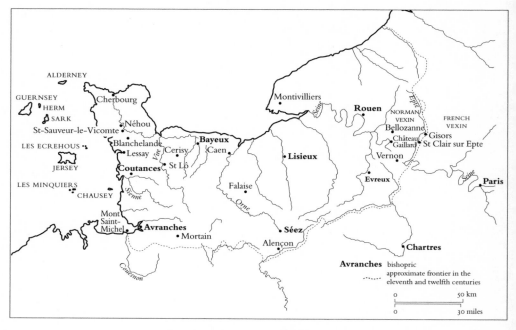

Normandy and the Channel Islands, 1204

CHAPTER TWO

Jersey before 1204

Gersui est pres de Costentin,
la u Normandie prent fin,
en mer est devers occident,
al fieu de Normandie apent.

Jersey is close to the Cotentin,
where Normandy comes to an end;
it is in the sea towards the west and
it belongs to the territory of Normandy.

(Master Wace, 'Roman de Rou', *c.* 1160)[1]

THUS the twelfth-century poet, Master Wace, himself a Jerseyman, succinctly portrayed the relationship between geography
and politics in the early history of Jersey. Jersey is defined in relation to the nearest part of the mainland, the Cotentin, and both are
subsumed in the political entity of the duchy of Normandy. This
chapter will examine the history of Jersey in the two hundred
years or so prior to 1204 and will demonstrate just how close were
the bonds between Jersey and the adjacent mainland.

Jersey is indeed close to the Cotentin, the strait being less than
30 kilometres (18 miles) at its narrowest. But the Channel Islands
may also be situated in a broader geographical context, the
'Western English Channel', defined by the West Country of
England to the north and Brittany and Lower Normandy to the
south. Within this region, the Channel Islands and others such as
the Isle of Wight represent the hilltops of land now submerged

which were finally divided from the mainland of Europe only about eight thousand years ago. From prehistoric times until the Anglo-Saxon and Viking invasions, a common culture and even political organization prevailed across the seaways of the Western English Channel. The relative ease of travel by sea in this region meant that the Channel Islands, throughout history, have never been isolated from the British Isles or Brittany. The fact that Jersey, in particular, lies very close to the coast of the Cotentin has nevertheless had the most important effect on its history. Contact with the adjacent mainland has always been possible for the Islanders, accustomed to sea travel, and hence there have always been close relations between the people of Jersey and of the Cotentin. With the demise of the cultural homogeneity of the Western English Channel, Jersey was bound to follow whatever developments occurred in the Cotentin, with the result that Jersey was absorbed first into the empire of the Franks, which reached its greatest extent under Charlemagne, and later into the dominion of the Scandinavian dukes of Normandy.

Jersey is the largest of the Channel Islands. In shape, it is roughly a rectangle, oriented east–west, approximately eight kilometres (5 miles) from north to south and fourteen kilometres (9 miles) from east to west, but with a deep indentation on the southern side, formed by St Aubin's Bay. In profile, the whole island seems to have been lifted up at the north coast, where the highest ground rises to nearly 150 metres (500 feet), and tilted gently, so that much of the land surface is one great south-facing slope. Long and deep valleys cut through the island, created by streams which run from the northern watershed, the steepest valleys thus running the short distance to the north coast, for instance at Grève de Lecq, the longest running all the way to

St Aubin's Bay in the south. The incidence of steep-sided valleys, mostly orientated north–south, makes east–west travel within the island difficult. Inaccessibility by land, added to the absence of natural harbours on the west coast and a less favourable climate and soil, meant that the western parts of the island were less populous and the communities there somewhat isolated compared with those in the east.

The difficulties presented by the topography were outweighed by the natural advantages of the island. The preponderance of well-drained, south-facing land, combined with the temperate climate, was ideal for agricultural production. The climate in the eleventh and twelfth centuries was even warmer and more temperate than it would be later in the Middle Ages. Grapes were on the menu of the eleventh-century residents of St Helier, as well as a variety of grains. Cereals were cultivated with such success that there was a surplus for export, while the steep valleys provided ideal sites for water-mills to grind the grain. Ready access to the sea on all sides encouraged a thriving fishing industry which provided a diet rich in seafoods of all types.

Before 1066

The close relations between Jersey and the Norman mainland were of long standing. From the end of the Roman Empire until the ninth century, the Channel Islands were subject to the same domination of the Gallo-Roman population by the Franks as was the adjacent mainland. The future duchy of Normandy was situated within the Frankish region of Neustria. Jersey was part of the empire of Charlemagne. Then, for a few decades after 850, it looked as though the Cotentin and the Islands might become part of the duchy of Brittany. During this period the Breton rulers of the Armorican peninsula successfully extended their authority over the Avranchin and Cotentin, including the Channel Islands. At the high point of Breton expansionism, the potential for Breton rule over the Channel Islands was thwarted by the combination of two factors – the fragmentation of political authority within Brittany and the destruction wrought across this region by Scandinavian raiders.

For the duration of the ninth and tenth centuries, the Channel Islands were vulnerable to attack from the Vikings, with neither the Breton nor the Frankish administration able to function even on the adjacent mainland. The bishops of Coutances were exiled in Rouen. All the monasteries of the Channel Islands, as in mainland Normandy, were abandoned or destroyed. Nevertheless, the rapid process of reorganization and rebuilding that occurred in Normandy in the early eleventh century suggests that there was some continuity of settlement and of Christian worship surviving from before the invasions. The establishment of Scandinavian, or Norman, rule in Rouen from 911 and subsequently in Lower Normandy, restored peace and stability to the Channel Islands.

Duke Robert 'the Magnificent' has the distinction of being the only duke of Normandy known to have visited Jersey at any time before 1204, and that unintentionally. The eleventh-century Norman chronicler, William of Jumièges, tells how at some time between 1033 and 1035 Duke Robert launched an expedition from Fécamp to invade England, but a storm blew the fleet off course and they landed at Jersey. 'At Jersey the fleet was detained a long time for a contrary wind kept blowing, so that in despair the duke became more and more distressed. Finally when he realized that he could in no way cross, he turned the prow and sailed homewards till they landed, as soon as possible, at Mont Saint-Michel.'[2]

The twelfth-century Jersey poet, Master Wace, retold this story in his vernacular history of the Norman dukes, the 'Roman de Rou'. Wace's more elaborate narrative displays his local knowledge:

> The wind was fair when they departed and they expected it
> to remain so. But.... The night became dark and black, the
> sky turned black and the sea became turbulent; the weather
> changed and the wind turned. They were unable to reach land
> or harbour; I do not know whether they were heading east or
> north... The storm and the north wind, which blew violently,
> troubled them so much that they could not reach land or
> return to Normandy. Yet they remained so close together that
> they came to the island of Jersey.

It is at this point that for the information of his audience Wace describes the situation of Jersey, in the passage quoted at the beginning of this chapter. Nevertheless, Wace continues, Duke Robert and his companions spent what seemed to them a long time in Jersey before Robert, impatient to resume campaigning, divided his fleet, sending part to the nearest coast of Brittany and crossing back to mainland Normandy himself.[3]

Once under the control of the dukes of Normandy, the Channel Islands were regarded as ducal 'domain'. That is, they were effectively the duke's private property, subject to his direct control. There was no powerful seigneur, lay or ecclesiastical, with a prior claim to any of the Islands to mediate the duke's authority there. In accordance with the customs and the exigencies of the times, however, the dukes promptly granted large portions away to be administered by others, both to reward their faithful men and to endow the Church. This is particularly apparent in Guernsey, which was divided in two halves, *c.* 1020, when Duke Robert gave one half to his faithful follower Nigel, the lord of Saint-Sauveur-le-Vicomte and *vicomte* of the Cotentin, and the other half to the *vicomte* of the Bessin, ancestor of the earls of Chester.

In Jersey, the picture is less clear. There were large areas of ducal domain on the island, but also estates held of the duke by Norman magnates. It is possible that Duke Robert gave a large share of Jersey, perhaps half of the island, to *vicomte* Nigel. This would explain the dominance of the abbey of Saint-Sauveur-le-Vicomte in Jersey, possessing five out of the twelve parish churches, as well as the priory of Bonnenuit, and a share in the tithes of all twelve parishes, and also why Nigel's heirs and their vassals were important landholders in Jersey in the twelfth century. If the *vicomtes* of the Cotentin did possess such a seigneurial monopoly, it had crumbled by 1100, leaving a number of aristocratic Norman families holding estates in Jersey by that date, as will be discussed in more detail in Chapter Four.

The sea between the Cotentin and the Channel Islands evidently did not represent a barrier to landholding in both places. This may be due in part to the fact that travel by water was more appealing in the Middle Ages than it is today, with the only made roads then being Roman ones. In a society in which individuals could maintain estates on both sides of the English Channel after 1066, the straits between Jersey and the Cotentin were of little account.

In the history of Jersey in the eleventh century, the dukes rather than the aristocracy play a leading role. Ducal dispositions of estates in the Channel Islands follow a pattern dictated by contemporary politics. The first phase occurred around 1025. This was the era when the Scandinavian 'counts of Rouen' had completed the extension of their regime over what was henceforth to be the medieval duchy of Normandy. In the west, this was at the expense of the counts of Rennes (the sometime dukes of Brittany), whose predecessors had occupied the Avranchin and part of the Cotentin. The frontier between Brittany and Normandy was fixed at the Couesnon. The early history of the abbey of Mont Saint-Michel, situated at the mouth of the river, represents this struggle. The earliest known benefactions to Mont Saint-Michel were by the counts of Rennes, but after 1000 patronage of the abbey was firmly in the hands of the Normans.

The earliest known ducal acts concerning the Channel Islands coincide with this, and manifest a deliberate policy of stamping Norman authority on Lower Normandy. The Norman dukes demonstrated their authority by giving land in alms to religious houses, as well as by dividing most of it up amongst their followers. Hence the generous donations by Duke Richard to the abbey of Mont Saint-Michel. On a similar scale is the endowment by Duke William II (the Conqueror) of the Norman abbey of Cerisy with possessions including two churches in Jersey.

It is probable that this is the period in which the twelve parishes of Jersey were created. The question of the origins of the parishes is one that cannot be answered with certainty in the present state of knowledge, so naturally theories abound. We would argue for a mid-eleventh-century date, and see the creation of the parishes by the Bishop of Coutances as an extension of the process of organization of the Channel Islands by the eleventh-century dukes of Normandy.

Some, if not all, of the parish churches were founded upon ancient religious sites that had been 'Christianized' in previous centuries. This does not, however, prove the antiquity of the parochial system. Some very prominent and conspicuously ancient religious sites, notably those of the chapel on La Hougue Bie and the chapel of Notre-Dame des Pas, did not become parish churches (plates 24, 25, 26). It is more probable that the sites of the present parish churches were among the many and various remains of the older ecclesiastical order, which had been disrupted but not totally destroyed by the Vikings. Around the mid-eleventh century, the bishop's officials surveyed what remained of Jersey's ecclesiastical infrastructure and selected sites that seemed appropriate from their location and perhaps the veneration in which they were still held by the populace, to rebuild and develop as parish churches. The religious sites rejected in this process either disappeared or were commemorated by the construction or reconstruction of simple chapels, such as the two just mentioned. Other early religious sites survived because in subsequent decades they were given to the religious orders to found monasteries. The most prestigious was the island site of the hermitage of St Helier, the site of the Augustinian abbey of St Helier (plate 29), but there were also old chapels (how old we do not know) at the core of the priories of Bonnenuit and Lecq, and possibly St Clement.

Further evidence for the comparatively late formation of the parishes can be derived from the secular administration – both the public administration of ducal government and the 'feudal system' of lay fiefs, the estates held of a lord, ultimately the duke, in return for homage and service. The latter do not coincide with parish boundaries. There is no strict correlation between parishes and fiefs in Jersey, and it is possible that the network of

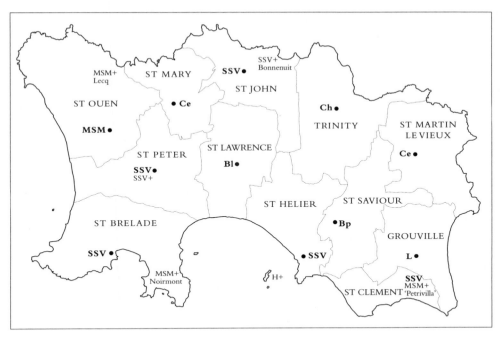

Jersey: parishes and patrons of churches, 1204

Priories

H+ Conventual priory of St Helier of the Islet (dependent on the abbey of Notre-Dame du Vœu, Cherbourg)

MSM+ Priory of the abbey of Mont Saint-Michel

SSV+ Priory of the abbey of Saint-Sauveur-le-Vicomte

Patrons of parish churches

Bl Abbot of Blanchelande

Bp Bishop of Coutances

Ce Abbot of Cerisy

Ch Abbot of Notre-Dame du Vœu, Cherbourg

L Abbot of Lessay

MSM Abbot of Mont Saint-Michel

SSV Abbot of Saint-Sauveur-le-Vicomte

parishes was overlaid onto an existing network of land-tenure. We have argued that the formation of the parishes was an ecclesiastical enterprise of the mid-eleventh century. The fiefs were a lay affair and probably originated somewhat earlier, since some of the parish churches were in the hands of laymen, that is, the lords of the estates on which the parish churches were established. As to ducal government, by the late twelfth century Jersey had been divided into three administrative districts, which royal clerks in Normandy called 'ministeria', roughly dividing the island into western, central and eastern sectors. Each ministerium appears to have contained four parishes, although we cannot be certain that the boundaries of ministeria and parishes were exactly coterminous. While an advocate of the antiquity of the parishes would see this as four existing parishes being combined into one ministerium, it is equally arguable that the ministeria were the older administrative units and that each came to be divided into four parishes, thus arriving at twelve parishes in total.

The earliest written records of parish churches support the theory that the parishes were established in the mid-eleventh century. The process had at least begun by 1042, when the young Duke William II, augmenting his father's gifts to the abbey of Cerisy, gave to the abbey 'in the island of Jersey two free churches, that is, the church of St Mary of the Burnt Monastery and [the church] of St Martin the Old, with their lands and one-third of the tithe of grain'.[4] By 'free', the scribe meant that the churches were not possessed by any layman, but evidently they were under ducal control. The attachment of tithes to the churches may indicate parochial organization. The creation of the parishes required the participation of the bishop of Coutances, and this was not feasible before the mid-eleventh century. During the tenth century, the bishops were exiled from Coutances, based at Rouen. They did not return until the episcopacy of Bishop Robert I (*c.* 1026–1048), who began to rebuild the cathedral of Coutances.

A co-ordinated programme of church-building in the mid-eleventh century is also suggested by the architecture of the twelve parish churches. The earliest stages of construction of the churches share common architectural features to such a degree that they must have been constructed to a common plan, and these features conform to the Anglo-Norman church architecture of the eleventh century. The typical Jersey parish church had stone walls reinforced with regularly spaced pilaster buttresses. Small, round-arched windows were set between the buttresses. The roof was wooden and covered with thatch. The church was cruciform and consisted of an unaisled nave and chancel, with short north and south transepts. The crossing supported a low, square tower with a saddleback roof, as can still be seen at St Lawrence and St Brelade (plates 21, 22, 27, 28). This initial uniformity was, then, largely responsible for the continued similarities in the medieval development of the parish churches, with their characteristic central towers, vaulted roofs and double naves.[5]

The credit for creating the parishes therefore probably belongs to Bishop Geoffrey de Montbray (1049–1093). Geoffrey not only finished rebuilding the cathedral but also reorganized the cathedral chapter, founded new monasteries in the Cotentin and was a valued counsellor of William the Conqueror. Bishop Geoffrey certainly took an interest in the Channel Islands: between 1049 and 1056 he obtained from Duke William the gift of the church of St Saviour for the cathedral of Coutances.

The process of creating the parishes was complete before Duke William's death in 1087, and possibly as early as 1066. This is apparent because the duke was generous in granting the tithes of Jersey churches to Norman abbeys: around 1066 he gave the nunnery of Holy Trinity, Caen, half of the tithes of six parishes of Jersey, and later he gave the nunnery of Montivilliers half of the tithe of the eight churches of St Clement, St Martin le Vieux, Grouville, St Helier, St Peter, St Brelade, St Ouen and St Mary.[6] The parishes missing from this list are St John, Trinity, St Lawrence and St Saviour. The reason for their omission is not necessarily that they did not then exist; the gift to Montivilliers of 'eight of the churches of Jersey' implies that there were others then in existence. St Saviour was certainly established before 1056, when the church with its tithes was given to the cathedral chapter of Coutances. This church and its appurtenances were jealously guarded by the archdeacons and their officials as a base for diocesan administration and hence were not awarded to any Norman monastery. St Lawrence too was unusual in being retained in the hands of the Norman king/duke until 1199, so it may be that the dukes did not wish to alienate any of this church's rights and revenues. Trinity Church may have a similar history, since it is first recorded when given to the newly founded abbey of St Helier by Henry II, between 1154 and 1172. St John, in contrast, was in 'private' hands. The parish church of St John is first mentioned *c.* 1140 by William de Vauville, whose father had given it to the abbey of Saint-Sauveur-le-Vicomte, so the church must have been in existence at least by the first quarter of the twelfth century.[7]

In addition to their essential spiritual and ecclesiastical role, the parishes became the basic units of community and of local government in Jersey. In a landscape of dispersed settlements, the parish church was the focal point, the hub of a network of lanes leading in from the farmsteads and hamlets of the parish. By the end of the thirteenth century, and probably dating back to the eleventh century, the parishes both regulated some of their own internal affairs, such as transfers of land, and dealt with the representatives of royal/ducal government (see Chapter Six).

The newly established order in the Cotentin in the mid-eleventh century, under both duke and bishop, is also reflected in ducal patronage of religious houses at Cherbourg. After 1066 Cherbourg acquired importance in communications and travel between Normandy and England. Shortly before 1066, Duke William reorganized the chapel of his castle of Cherbourg into a college of secular canons. These were then at the duke's service to minister to the religious needs of the denizens of the castle and the ducal entourage when they visited, and also to provide clerical services to the ducal administration (one of the canons was Duke William's chaplain, Odo 'Saillutra'). Among grants of land in Cherbourg and its environs to constitute livings for the canons, the duke gave from the ducal domain in Guernsey the church of St Martin de la Bellouse and one hundred acres of land in the same parish. The courtier William de Vauville gave from his own domain the church of Alderney and arable land on the island, as well as revenue from his mills in Guernsey and grants from his estates in Equeurdreville on the mainland. At the dedication of the new collegiate church, Duke William added a gift of land in Jersey, a parcel of arable land in the parish of St Saviour.[8] The symmetry between Duke William's near-contemporary patronage of the cathedral of Coutances and the collegiate church of Cherbourg cannot be coincidental. Each was given a parish church, one in

Jersey and one in Guernsey, and at the ceremony of dedication, a further gift of one ploughland on the other island; and *both* were given the church of Alderney, giving rise to a dispute which was decided in favour of the cathedral by Henry I in 1134.

At the same time, the town of Caen was established. Having gained control of Lower Normandy, the dukes sought to consolidate their authority by developing Caen as a second capital of the duchy. In the charter that records Duke William founding the abbey of Holy Trinity, Caen, around 1066, the endowments listed include one ploughland and a mill in Jersey, and the half of the tithes of six parishes mentioned above. A few years later, William and his wife Matilda designated the uses to which the nuns should put their revenues, with those from the alms in Jersey designated for the nuns' food. Finally, Duke William confirmed the nuns' possessions in Jersey, adding that his chaplain, Reginald, on becoming a monk, had surrendered the land and tithes he held of the duke in Jersey, which were now given to Holy Trinity, Caen.[9] William the Conqueror's endowment of Holy Trinity with tithes in Jersey resembles his benefaction for the nuns of Montivilliers. Between 1068 and 1076, William confirmed the endowments of his father Duke Robert, the founder of Montivilliers, and added for the first time possessions in Lower Normandy. Williams's gift to Montivillers of half of eight churches in Jersey again stipulated that the revenue was to be used for the nuns' food.[10] As with the duke's patronage of the secular canons of Coutances and Cherbourg, these benefactions to the nuns are so similar it is tempting to see a deliberate plan at work.

This analysis of ducal patronage of Norman religious houses demonstrates that from the early eleventh century the dukes of

Normandy were active patrons, even founders, of religious houses situated in the Cotentin. They were lavish with benefactions of lands and rights there, and the Channel Islands were no exception. An endowment of some land and rights in one or more of the Islands was commonly made simultaneously with grants of land and rights on the mainland. Possessions in the Islands were clearly desirable. It may be that, as noted above, people thought so little of crossing the sea to Jersey that they did not distinguish between possessions on the mainland and in Jersey, and in the case of the Islands, the dukes had plenty to give. Additionally, the many references to agriculture, cereals and water-mills in these endowments, even the specific use of possessions in Jersey for provision of food for the religious, suggest that Jersey was a valuable source of cereals.

While the broad outline of Jersey's political history in this period is relatively clear – political sovereignty by the dukes of Normandy, ecclesiastical authority by the bishop of Coutances – we know very little about lay lordship and land tenure before 1066.

1066–1154: the Anglo-Norman realm

The Norman conquest of England did not have a direct effect upon the Channel Islands, because they were already part of Normandy. The indirect effects were, however, both critical in the long term and favourable to Jersey's fortunes. The Islands were more secure after 1066 when England and Normandy were united under Norman rule. At the same time the possibility of renewed invasion from Brittany was diminished by the continuing internal weakness of the Breton ducal regime and the success of the Anglo-Norman rulers. The sons of William the Conqueror who succeeded him in the duchy do not seem to have shared their father's interest in the Channel Islands. There are no known acts of ducal patronage involving Jersey from *c.* 1080 until after 1154. This may have been simply because Duke William had reasserted ducal authority in Lower Normandy so thoroughly and successfully. It may also have been an effect of the union of England and Normandy, which meant that the Channel Islands were no longer a political frontier.

In contrast with the period before 1066, there is considerably more evidence for the landholding families in Jersey in the twelfth century, although it is still fragmentary. The Carteret family first appears in the documentary record in 1125, although the family which took its name from Carteret on the Cotentin coast may have possessed land in Jersey long before that date. In 1125 Reginald de Carteret gave property in Jersey to the abbey of Mont Saint-Michel. The land must have been in the north-west of the island, since this endowment developed into the priory of Lecq, demonstrating that the Carteret family were already in possession of land in the parish of St Ouen by 1125. A confirmation of this grant made in 1135 by Reginald's heir refers to the site of his nearby 'curia', the centre for administration of the estate by the lord or his estate officials.[11]

The Wac or Wake family also appear in the twelfth century. Master Wace, the poet, was born in Jersey between 1090 and 1110. Although 'Wace' was probably the poet's personal name, it is possible he was a member of this family. Hugh Wake, a near-contemporary of Master Wace, was a tenant of Ranulf II, Earl of Chester and *vicomte* of the Bessin, holding land of the earl in the Bessin (at Longues) and in Guernsey (in the 'fief le Comte'). Earl Ranulf's patronage made the family's fortunes when he gave Hugh in marriage the heiress of the honour of Bourne (Lincolnshire) in the mid-1140s, and Hugh Wake and his descendants belatedly entered the class of Anglo-Norman cross-Channel landholders. Unlike most Norman tenants, their Channel Island estates were important to the Wake family. This was especially so after the death of Earl Ranulf, when Henry II gave the whole of the 'fief le Comte' in Guernsey to Hugh Wake, making his estates the largest of any lay tenant in the island. The family also possessed some land in Jersey. Roger Wake, Hugh's brother, held land in the parish of St John, *c.* 1150. Richard Wake, a priest, was in dispute with the abbey of Saint-Sauveur over property in the parish of St Helier in 1180.[12] In the early thirteenth century, certain land in Jersey was deemed to be in 'the fief of Baldwin Wake'.

In the first half of the twelfth century, there is some evidence for the structure of feudal tenure in Jersey. As noted above, the tenants-in-chief were Norman aristocrats whose estates in the Channel Islands represented only a small proportion of their total landholdings. It appears that in the next level of the feudal hierarchy, the tenants who held land in Jersey of the tenants-in-chief were themselves predominantly Norman landholders. As discussed in Chapter Four, they possessed estates comprising lands, revenues and rights, both in the Cotentin and in the Channel Islands.

Examples of families of any substance whose only possessions were in Jersey, or even in the Islands, are not forthcoming. In the mid-twelfth century, one Baldwin son of Adam held some land in the parish of St John of the fief of William de Vauville. The absence of a toponymic from the Cotentin leaves open the possibility that Baldwin was someone whose principal tenement was his estate in Jersey, but we cannot be certain. This obscurity is due to the nature of the documentary sources: the families with interests on the mainland patronized monasteries on the mainland, which in turn preserved records of their donations in the monastic archives. For evidence of families based in Jersey, with no substantial interests on the mainland, different sources are required, and these do not appear until a later period.

The period between 1066 and 1135 was one of comparative peace and prosperity in the Channel Islands, which benefited from the security of the surrounding seas being united under a single authority. On the other hand, it was a period in which the Islands remained politically obscure. Ducal interest in Cherbourg, at least, was revived after the death of Henry I in 1135, during the period when Duke William's granddaughter, Matilda 'the Empress', and her husband Geoffrey Plantagenet, Count of Anjou, ruled Normandy, with their son Henry aspiring to succeed to the kingdom of England. Matilda founded a house of Augustinian canons known as Notre-Dame du Vœu near Cherbourg, an abbey which was to be very important to the history of Jersey.

1154–1199: the Plantagenet empire

The year 1154 was arguably of greater significance for the Channel Islands than 1066 had been. The 'Plantagenet empire' came into being with extraordinary swiftness between 1152 and 1154, as described in Chapter One. The well-established political unit of England and Normandy, the 'Anglo-Norman realm', was re-oriented to look outwards, particularly towards the south. One consequence was a growth in sea travel between the northern and southern dominions, by royal servants and by merchants enjoying the commercial opportunities opened up by this new trading zone. The Channel Islands acquired a new significance as a landfall for ships from Ireland and the south coast of England to the Continent, and ships rounding Finistère from the south.

By the 1190s there is evidence for the production of dried fish on an industrial scale.[13] This activity was a ducal monopoly in the Channel Islands. The duke, or other seigneur to whom the duke had granted this privilege, supplied land near the seashore where the fishing boats landed their catch, and the wooden frames (called 'esperkeria' because the long poles measured one perch in length) which were the necessary infrastructure. In return, he obliged his tenants to dry their fish there, for a fee. In typical medieval fashion, the activity of fish-drying, the seigneurial monopoly over it and the revenue derived therefrom all came to be known by the same word, 'esperkeria', later *éperquerie*. By 1199, the farm of the duke's 'esperkeria' for Guernsey and Jersey totalled 50 *livres angevins*, which means the annual revenue was expected to equal or exceed this amount.

In keeping with the Channel Islands' new importance, Henry II may have encouraged the urban and economic development of Jersey. This seems to have been the intention of the king's foundation of the abbey of St Helier, situated on the Islet in St Aubin's Bay, as a house of Augustinian canons. Regular canons such as these were not cloistered monks who rejected the world. As well as offering spiritual ministry, their pastoral work among the local population typically involved providing comfort for the poor, the sick and travellers, and they would even act as scribes for the few who had need of the written word. The introduction of Augustinian canons to Jersey in the mid-twelfth century, and in particular to St Helier, could have been prompted by an increase in population and commercial activity, itself the result of the peace and prosperity brought to Jersey by its position within the Plantagenet dominions.

Old Street, on the west side of the present town centre, was already 'le Vieux Chemin' by the eighteenth century, when it was a narrow, winding lane with few buildings. The scene was very different in the second half of the twelfth century, as this part of St Helier seems to have been the site of urban development, perhaps connected with the foundation of the abbey. Excavations on the south side of Old Street in the 1970s revealed an aisled hall-house, with stone walls and a thatched roof, built not long before 1185.[14] The water-mill given to the canons by Henry II as part of the abbey's endowment may have been situated nearby. Although it is usually assumed that the mill of the abbey of St Helier was the later Town Mill, some distance north of the parish church, the 'Faux Bie' watercourse, running to the south of the Old Street house, is also said to have been the site of a mill belonging to the canons of the Islet. It may be that the water-mill and the 'marsh of St Helier' given by Henry II were both situated west of the parish church, and that the king intended urban development of this area. The old market-place, known as 'the king's market-place' ('forum regis') by 1299, is also situated in this part of the town of St Helier, originally almost on the medieval shoreline between Old Street (a little further inland from the shore) and the parish church to the east. It has been said that Henry II's endowment of the new abbey included the right to hold a market, a valuable source of cash revenue. There is, however, no contemporary evidence of such a grant, rather it seems the market remained in the king's hands. By 1309, there were at least ninety-two taverners and bakers in the parish of St Helier, compared with an average of twenty-six in each of the other parishes.[15] All this provides evidence for urban development of St Helier in the late twelfth and thirteenth centuries, which was at the outset promoted by Henry II.

Little is known about the administration of Jersey under the dukes of Normandy in the twelfth century. However, the Channel Islands seem to have been administered in the same way as other parts of Normandy, so more can be surmised. The ducal domain, the land within the duke's direct control but normally cultivated by free tenants, was administered by royal officials, as described in Chapter One (see p. 25). The land held as fiefs, or in alms by the church, was administered by the lay or ecclesiastical seigneurs, each of whom was responsible for rendering military service and financial 'aids' to the duke when required to do so.

Fragmentary records of the Norman Exchequer at Caen have survived, dating from the years between 1180 and 1204. These, and a few references in charters, are our only evidence for the administration of Jersey in this period. This evidence is so meagre that it is not possible to understand or reconstruct the institutions of government as a whole. Nevertheless, two conclusions can be drawn from this material. One is that the Channel Islands were regarded as a separate administrative unit or units for the purposes of ducal government; they were not part of any administrative district on the adjacent mainland. The second is that the officials exercising ducal authority in the Islands were local men, with interests in the Islands and in the Cotentin. With the exception of the royal justices, who visited from time to time, the officials were not imposed from outside.

The year for which we have the most evidence is 1180 because of a remarkable coincidence. First, there is the unique survival of a charter made as the record of a sitting of the royal court in Guernsey in 1179. Second, one of the few surviving records ('rolls') of the Exchequer of Normandy is that of the session of the Exchequer held at Michaelmas 1180. This is the only extant roll of the Norman Exchequer which contains an account for Jersey (there are accounts for Guernsey in the fragments from 1195 and 1198). Taken together, these two sources permit a 'snapshot' view of the administration of Jersey in 1179–80. The Exchequer roll shows that William de Courcy, the Seneschal of Normandy, had held Jersey and Guernsey at farm until his death in 1176. A man of such status would not have had any personal involvement in the administration, rather this office would have represented a means of rewarding him for his service as Seneschal. William would have employed deputies to collect the ducal revenues due from the Islanders and to make sure these exceeded the annual farm and hence yielded a profit. The 1180 Exchequer roll names Robert Agneaux as the late William de Courcy's representative, attending the Exchequer to account for the 200 *livres angevins* 'from the Islands' still owed by William de Courcy's heirs.

By Michaelmas 1180 it appears that this had all changed. At this time Jersey was divided into the three ministeria, whose boundaries ran generally north–south. Guernsey was accounted for as a single unit. Jersey's westernmost sector was known as Crapoudoit, 'the toad-stream', identified with St Peter's Valley. The central sector was Groceium, probably connected with the fief 'as Grouchees' in Trinity parish. The easternmost was Gorroic, from which is derived the modern 'Gorey'. As mentioned above, there is no way of knowing the antiquity of this division. It might have been ancient, pre-dating the creation of the parishes, or it might have been very recent, part of the widespread governmental reforms of Henry II in the 1160s and 1170s, a time when the foundation of St Helier's abbey shows that the king was interested in Jersey's development. This tripartite division of Jersey for administrative purposes does not appear

Extract concerning Jersey from the roll of the Exchequer of Normandy, 1180 anywhere in contemporary sources other than the 1180 Exchequer roll. There is, however, a hint of the ministerium of Groceium in testimony given in 1309, that the king's stocks for keeping prisoners from the parishes of St Lawrence, St John, Trinity and St Helier should be maintained in the fief 'as Grouchees' in Trinity.[16]

In 1180 each ministerium was held at farm by a different individual – Richard Burnouf, Roger Godel and Gislebert de la Hougue respectively. Unlike William de Courcy, these were not important magnates or courtiers; they were local men participating in ducal government. All three appear to have held land in their respective ministeria, or at least their descendants did. This development may not have been such a radical change as it at first appears. Probably the men named in the 1180 Exchequer roll as the farmers of Guernsey and the three ministeria of Jersey had held these offices for years, as William de Courcy's deputies. On his demise, they were promoted to the position of accounting personally for their own circumscriptions to the Exchequer.

It is tempting to confer on Gislebert de la Hougue some superiority in the ducal administration of Jersey and Guernsey. Gislebert's ministerium of Gorroic included the site of the future Mont Orgueil castle, but there is no evidence that the headquarters of the ducal administration in Jersey was situated on this site before the construction of the castle. More significant is the fact that in 1180 Gislebert not only accounted for Gorroic, but also for the whole of Guernsey, where he had a deputy, Robert de Haverlant. The charter of 1179, mentioned above, records Gislebert de la Hougue acting as *vicomte* ('vicecomes'), presiding over the royal court in Guernsey.

Gislebert de la Hougue is first recorded in 1156, when he attested two acts of Robert de Torigny, abbot of Mont Saint-Michel, during the abbot's visit to Jersey that year. Somewhat before 1172, in attesting a charter of Jordan de Barneville for the abbey of St Helier, Gislebert's name appears immediately before that of Robert de Haverlant. Since the latter was Gislebert's deputy in Guernsey in 1180, this attestation would seem to have been made in their capacities as royal officials. Unhelpfully, but not atypically, their attestations are not accompanied by any official titles. Gislebert is not recorded after 1180, not unreasonably since he had been active in the administration of the Channel Islands since 1156. In 1195 and 1198, the account for Guernsey was rendered at the Exchequer by Robert de Sainte-Mère-Eglise, who was perhaps Gislebert's successor in Jersey as well.

The Exchequer roll of 1180 contains valuable information about the financial administration of Jersey in that year. The farm of the ministerium of Groceium was 140 *livres angevins*, while Crapoudoit and Gorroic were each assessed at 160 *livres angevins*. This gives an indication of their value to the Crown: the royal revenues to be collected from each ministerium were expected to equal or exceed the amount of the farm. By way of comparison, in 1180 the farm of Guernsey was 200 *livres angevins*, the farm of the *prévôté* of Falaise was 480 *livres angevins*, the farm of the *vicomté* of Coutances was 50 *livres angevins* and the farm of Tinchebrai was 100 *livres angevins*. Jersey, with a total farm of 460 *livres angevins*, was therefore a comparatively large source of royal revenue. The Islanders also paid hearth-tax ('focagium', *fouage*) to the duke of Normandy, at least from the reign of Henry II and probably from an earlier period. This tax was levied every three years, customarily, by the dukes of Normandy and survived in the Channel Islands long after 1204.

In addition to the regular revenues, the 1180 Exchequer roll records other types of payment into the royal/ducal treasury. One category of revenue itemized is 'reliefs', payments due to the Crown when a tenant-in-chief's heir wished to enter his or her inheritance. In 1180, several Jersey tenants are named in this capacity, including William le Gallichan, who had to pay 6 *livres angevins* to enter his fief in Groceium (evidently the family already held its fief in Trinity parish). Similarly, the chattels of individuals might be forfeited, and thence released to another who undertook to pay a lump sum for them. In Crapoudoit, Humphrey of 'Mara', a priest, paid to have the chattels of Ranulf de L'Etacq. Robert son of Vitalis paid to have the chattels of his late brother, forfeited because the deceased was accused of usury. Another source of revenue was the income from land which had been taken into the king's hand due to the death or default of the tenant. In Groceium, the land of Richard the Norman and Pagan, worth 10 s. *angevin per annum*, was in the king's hand because the pair had been convicted of some wrongdoing and hanged. In Gorroic, the garden of Robert Malet rendered 30 s. while it was in the king's hand (for reasons unstated).

Last, but certainly not least, were the payments incurred in connection with the exercise of royal/ducal justice. For example, in Groceium, Richard 'Normant' (the same man who was hanged?) was liable to pay 30 s. for having a record of the outcome of a trial by battle. Unspecified judicial fines, known as 'amercements', were owed by Gislebert 'Imperator' (Lemprière) in Groceium, by William the priest and Eudo Azor in Crapoudoit, and by one Waldrain in Gorroic. The 'farmers' of each of the three ministeria also farmed the numerous amercements due after each visit of the royal justices. In 1180 there was no new farm of amercements.

ETVENIT AD PEVENESÆ :‑

1. The Bayeux Tapestry (detail). In 1066 the Norman invading fleet crossed the Channel – the beginning of the political union of the Channel Islands with England.

14. Effigy of Henry II. The king was laid to rest at the abbey of Fontevraud, in the Loire valley, the heartland of the Plantagenet dynasty.

15. Effigy of King John. Having lost most of his Continental lands, John was buried in England, in Worcester Cathedral.

The three farmers, however, were all accounting for and paying off the 'old farm of amercements', presumably that assessed when the royal justices last visited the Islands to conduct their assizes.

If the financial administration of the officials in Jersey was overseen by the Exchequer at Caen, in judicial matters they were subject to royal justices who visited the Islands every few years to exercise royal/ducal jurisdiction. Royal justices led by Ralph de Valmont visited Jersey at some time during the reign of Henry II, although no records of the proceedings of these courts have survived. The Norman Exchequer roll of 1195 refers to three royal legates ('missi'), Herbert the clerk, Richard de 'Osolvilla' and Richard 'Bervuche', sent from Coutances to 'the Islands' to conduct inquests about escheats, that is, to ascertain by sworn evidence from local men what property ought to be forfeited to the king due to the death or default of the tenant. These legates were royal servants charged with collecting information on a particular subject, rather than justices determining legal matters, but their mission demonstrates that the administration of Jersey was directed from mainland Normandy.

Occasional visits by justices would not have met the needs of the population for law and order. They must have had access to justice more regularly, and this appears to have been supplied by the same officials who farmed the ministeria. The 1179 charter discussed above records Gislebert de la Hougue as *vicomte*, presiding over the royal court in Guernsey. The existence of this charter, authenticated by the attachment of Gislebert's seal (plate 11), does not necessarily mean that Gislebert had a monopoly on royal/ducal justice in the Channel Islands. The 1180 Exchequer roll provides ample evidence that the other two officials in Jersey, Richard Burnouf and Roger Godel, also exercised jurisdiction within their respective ministeria. All three (as well as Robert de Haverlant in Guernsey) were fined for having exceeded their authority by conducting judicial proceedings that were reserved for the royal justices. These included 'concordia de meihaimato' (literally 'settlement of maiming', where parties involved in an assault had reached a compromise) and administering the judicial ordeal of hot iron. This implies that there were certain judicial proceedings which *were* properly within the jurisdiction of these local officials, but that sometimes they acted over-zealously and exceeded their judicial authority.

1199–1204: the reign of King John

On to this busy scene of Plantagenet exploitation of the Channel Islands was imposed, in the 1190s, the lordship of the future King John. The lands given to John to rule as a junior member of the royal family formed a territorial pattern into which the Channel Islands fitted naturally. Once again, the 'Western English Channel' emerges as a region. First, John had been made Lord of Ireland by his father in 1185. His marriage to the heiress of the earldom of Gloucester, arranged at around the same time, brought him interests in the south-west of England and especially the flourishing port of Bristol. In 1189, on his accession, Richard I gave John vast estates in northern England and on both sides of the Western English Channel: the honour of Mortain, which was comprised of estates in the Avranchin, the Cotentin (including land in the port of Barneville, near Jersey), Devon and Cornwall; the castellany of Sainte-Mère-Eglise; and the counties of Devon, Cornwall, Dorset and Somerset.

It would be reasonable to assume that the Channel Islands were given to John in 1189 along with all the other generous endowments in Normandy and England, especially in view of the geography of John's possessions. Contemporary sources, however, make no mention of this. The first dated reference to John in connection with the Islands is from the Norman Exchequer roll of September 1198, which records that the farm of Guernsey was not paid into the royal treasury but was diverted to John. John is not mentioned in the surviving account for Guernsey in 1195, which suggests that he acquired lordship of Guernsey, and presumably also of Jersey, between 1195 and 1198. There exists only one single charter of Richard I directly relating to the Channel Islands, in which the King confirms the right of the abbey of Mont Saint-Michel to 'wreck of the sea' in the monks' lands in Jersey and Guernsey, dated May 1198.[17] This royal act would not be inconsistent with John holding the Islands, or at least their revenues, of his brother the King at the time. We do not know, therefore, when John became Lord of the Channel Islands; possibly in 1189, certainly by September 1198.

Count John's tenure of Jersey and Guernsey was the first time that lordship of the Islands as a group had been vested in any individual other than the duke of Normandy. It is probable that this innovation caused little change to the administrative institutions of the Channel Islands, except that John was interposed as lord between the Island tenants and the Crown.

Evidently John took some interest in his lordship of Jersey, using his possessions in the Islands to exercise religious patronage. The grant of the parish church of St Lawrence to the abbey of Blanchelande saw the disposal of the last church of which the king/duke had remained patron. Out of the royal domain, now John's own, he granted to the abbey of Bellozanne rents totalling 20 *livres* from tenements in the valley that now bears the abbey's name, extending from the lands of William de Surville (the future Surville manor) down to the seashore. Some of John's household knights were recruited from his Mortain lands, perhaps even from the Channel Islands; Richard de Carteret and Ingeram de Furnet were both younger sons of families that held manors in Jersey as well as in the Cotentin.

On the succession of King John in 1199, the Channel Islands reverted to the status of royal/ducal domain. It was not long before John alienated them, though. In January 1200, he gave a favoured Norman courtier, Peter de Préaux, the islands of Jersey, Guernsey and Alderney as a fief to hold for the service of three knights. At first this was only a temporary arrangement, until John could arrange the marriage of Peter to a wealthy heiress, namely the daughter of the lord of the Isle of Wight. Presumably John intended the Islands to revert to royal domain upon Peter's marriage. Six months later, in June, John issued a second charter on the subject, this time to the effect that, if Peter should die before he married a suitable heiress, then his tenure of the Channel Islands would be deemed hereditary and would pass to Peter's heirs (presumably his brothers or nephews).

Peter, one of the five brothers of Préaux who were companions of Richard I and John in turn, was high in John's favour. Like John before him, Peter was normally absent from the Channel Islands, if he ever visited at all, and governed through deputies. These could be local men, such as Reginald de Carteret, who acted as a royal official to collect a levy for the defence of the Islands when the Capetian threat loomed in 1202. Peter did have at least some knowledge of the institutions of royal/ducal government he had supplanted. In a charter for the benefit of the abbey of Saint-Sauveur-le-Vicomte, Peter offers the abbey 'the tithes which the officials of the Islands were anciently accustomed to take in the parishes of the Islands, each according to his right and his due portion, defined as the tithe of one plot in each parish…'.[18] The tradition of using estates in the Islands to patronize monasteries on the Norman mainland continued, now for the benefit of the Cistercian abbey of Le Val-Richer. This abbey must have had some significance to Peter personally, since it had no other connection with the Cotentin. Peter gave Le Val-Richer the only habitable island in the Ecréhous archipelago, where the monks were to build a church in honour of God and the Virgin Mary, 'that the Divine mystery might be celebrated each day'. Later evidence suggests that the monks also performed the very practical function of maintaining a beacon for shipping. The monks' harsh existence was alleviated by other gifts made by Peter de Préaux and others, including a water-mill in the parish of St Saviour and land at Archirondel where the prior built a house.[19]

This chapter began with an account of what little we know of the history of Jersey in the early Middle Ages. Then the Channel Islands, on the very edge of the Carolingian empire, were exposed to attack from Bretons and Vikings. But by 1204 the islands had enjoyed some two hundred years of peace and prosperity under the firm rule of the dukes of Normandy. The fact that they were separated from the mainland did not hinder the Islanders from joining in the flourishing life of the duchy. The seas separating the islands from the Cotentin presented no obstacle to a dynasty of dukes and aristocrats and their attendant courtiers, bureaucrats, churchmen, warriors and merchants, who were accustomed to seafaring, even across the English Channel. With a favourable climate and access to the riches of the sea, the Islanders produced an abundance of cereals and fish, which they traded in a thriving commerce with the nearby mainland. The Norman dukes, unsurprisingly, maintained their authority over Jersey. Whether lay or ecclesiastical, the various Norman landholders held their fiefs of the ruler, with large tracts and valuable rights, such as *éperquerie*, retained in the king/duke's hands.

The political fortunes of the Channel Islands nevertheless did not rest unchanged over this period. In the decades after the year 1000, the dukes of Normandy took a keen interest in the tenure of land in the islands, whether by the Church or by Norman aristocrats, as part and parcel of their drive to dominate the Cotentin. Under the Anglo-Norman rulers, from 1066 to 1154, the islands were secure and seemingly of more interest to the Norman clergy and aristocrats who had acquired estates there. With the advent of the Plantagenet dynasty, whose territorial interests lay as much in Aquitaine as in Normandy and England, the Channel Islands acquired a new logistical significance as a landfall for shipping between north and south. From this period there are signs of renewed economic development in Jersey, promoted by Henry II. A further change occurred when John, Count of Mortain, was given lordship of the Channel Islands, and later gave the Islands to a trusted Norman courtier. In 1200, no one would have predicted that the peace and security enjoyed for so long by the Islanders was about to be threatened.

CHAPTER THREE
The fight for Jersey,
1204–1217

THE SUCCESS OR FAILURE of the Plantagenet regime depended upon the individual decisions of all the Channel Island
tenants. Since there was no lord or representative body with the
power to accept or reject Plantagenet sovereignty on behalf of the
population, each individual effectively had the right to decide
whether he would support the Plantagenet regime or go over to
the Capetian side. Each had to decide for himself whether his best
interests lay in supporting the Plantagenets and forfeiting his land
in Normandy, or supporting the Capetians and forfeiting his land
in the Islands. The ultimate success of the Plantagenet regime was
due to the fact that, by the mid-thirteenth century, all the remaining Jersey tenants had their principal landed interests, and an
elevated social and political status, in the Channel Islands. They
had no interest in political reunion with Normandy. But this consequence was not inevitable and almost certainly not foreseen in
1204 or for some years afterwards. In this period, the foundations
were laid for the eventual success of the Plantagenet regime in the
policies of King John and the regents of Henry III. These involved
determined military action against Capetian invasion and sanctions imposed internally against potential rebellion, combined
with positive steps to minimize disruption and to make the
Islanders as secure and prosperous as possible in the changed circumstances. This chapter will chronicle the events of 1204 and the
immediate aftermath as they affected Jersey, and examine the
response of the Plantagenet regime.[1] The following chapters will
examine in more detail continuity and change in the landholding

79

classes, in ecclesiastical organization, and in law and government, the factors which encouraged the formation of the native Jersey elite.

The events of 1204 to 1217

We are accustomed to the idea that, with the loss of Normandy, Jersey 'became' a special dominion under Plantagenet sovereignty; indeed the year 2004 is held to mark the 800th anniversary of this event. It comes as something of a surprise, then, that in the summer of 1204 the Channel Islands fell to the Capetians at the same time as mainland Normandy. The only difference was that King John promptly launched a campaign to regain the Islands and eventually succeeded. In proceedings before royal justices in Jersey in 1309, sworn evidence was given that:

> A certain king of France disinherited the Lord John, formerly King of England, of the duchy of Normandy and then the said King of France on two occasions ejected the said Lord John the King from these islands and occupied them as annexed to the said duchy. And the said Lord John the King with armed force on two occasions reconquered these islands from the said King of France. And from that his said second conquest he and his posterity Kings of England have held these islands up to the present.[2]

Nearly one hundred years had elapsed since the 'second conquest', and this testimony could be dismissed as lacking the authority of personal recollection, but evidence from other sources suggests that this bald narrative is essentially accurate. King John's representatives were 'ejected' from the Channel Islands by the rival Capetian forces twice, first in 1204 and a second time in

1216. On both occasions, the Plantagenets successfully counter-attacked and reconquered the Islands within a matter of months.

1204: the Capetian conquest

The security of the Channel Islands, along with the rest of Normandy, was threatened from 1202, when Philip Augustus pronounced John's Continental dominions forfeit (see p. 34). John was quick to see the strategic importance of the Channel Islands, perhaps as a result of his lordship of the Islands and the Western English Channel in the 1190s. On 22 July 1202, at Rouen, King John issued three writs addressed to his faithful men of Jersey, Guernsey and Alderney, ordering them to aid his royal servants in keeping custody of the Islands, defending against foreigners and capturing anyone from the lands of the King's enemies, and ejecting known malefactors from the Islands.[3] Thus the men of Jersey received a personal and direct mandate from their former lord, now the king, to stand ready and take precautions in preparation for defence of the island against a Capetian invasion. For the time being, that was sufficient.

By the summer of 1203, the prospects of war were becoming more imminent. In July, John issued a mandate to Peter de Préaux, as Lord of the Islands, ordering that the fiefholders of Jersey and Guernsey should levy from their men a reasonable 'aid' to defend the islands from foreigners. The funds raised would be used to sustain the defending knights and soldiers. This suggests that garrisons had already been established in these islands. The mandate does not appear to require military service from the fiefs, only money. The tenants-in-chief were to levy whatever they deemed reasonable from their own tenants and render it to Reginald de Carteret, acting as a royal official in this instance. This measure

appears not to have been effective, or if it was executed, then insuf-
ficient funds were raised. Three weeks later, John issued a further
mandate specifying who was liable and for how much. Collection
was not to be left to the tenants-in-chief; the new mandate was
addressed to Peter de Préaux's officials of Jersey and Guernsey,
ordering them to execute it. It stipulated that all landholders in
Jersey and Guernsey, whether lay or ecclesiastical, were liable:
'bishops, abbots, abbesses, clergy, knights, vavassours and others
who have revenues and tenements in Jersey and Guernsey', and
also the amount, one-fifth of their annual revenue, whether they
held in fief or in alms.[4]

The events of the next few months demonstrate that John's
grant of the Islands to Peter de Préaux as a fief had been a mistake,
and on two grounds. First, it was a mistake in principle. The
absence of any magnate possessing a controlling share in Jersey or
Guernsey had always been greatly to the advantage of the dukes of
Normandy, and it would be again. But just at the time when lordship of the Islands really mattered, John had alienated them from
royal domain and placed them all in the hands of one man, Peter
de Préaux. When Rouen fell in June 1204, and Peter was obliged
to surrender all his lands to Philip Augustus, 'his lands' included
the Channel Islands. According to the principles of feudal relationships, which he was in the process of inventing, Philip
Augustus could then rightfully take possession of the Islands.
John's mistake in giving the Channel Islands to Peter de Préaux
was compounded by the fact that Peter was not a man of the
Cotentin. His family were of the lesser aristocracy from near
Rouen. Peter and his brothers had risen to unexpected heights
through service to the Plantagenets, and therefore in a sense owed
them everything, but equally they wished to preserve their

patrimony. Thus John de Préaux, the oldest and hence the heir of the patrimony, went over to Philip Augustus and was actively assisting Philip Augustus's campaign in Normandy while Peter was leading the Plantagenet defence of Rouen. The brothers seem to have maintained a cordial relationship, at least once Peter had come to terms with Philip Augustus, because John gave his son as a hostage for Peter's good conduct. The immediate fate of the Channel Islands was thus determined far away in Rouen, by a 'lord of the Islands' with little or no interest in their fate. The Islanders themselves could have resisted the Capetian representatives when they came to take possession, perhaps they did, but they were effectively leaderless by that time and evidently any resistance was unsuccessful.

From August 1203, there is a period of just over two years for which we have no documentary evidence of events in the Channel Islands, but in this period the whole of the duchy of Normandy was conquered by the Capetian forces, generally with the Norman tenants being unable or unwilling to resist. As noted above, the Channel Islands could have been delivered to Philip Augustus quite legitimately. Peter de Préaux held the Islands in fief right up until the loss of Normandy. In May 1204, Peter was one of the defenders of the city of Rouen and his name appears at the top of the list of laymen in the document recording the terms of their capitulation to Philip Augustus in June.[5] One of the terms was that the defenders would be permitted to go free if they rendered homage to the Capetian king for their lands in Normandy. Any lands thus transferred would have passed to Capetian sovereignty without force and with the consent of their tenant-in-chief. In the case of Peter de Préaux, the lands in question included Jersey, Guernsey and Alderney.

What actually happened as regards lordship of the Channel Islands in the summer of 1204 is not known. The surrender of Peter de Préaux meant that they came under Capetian rule. Did Peter continue to hold the Islands in fief of Philip Augustus? He did not return to the service of King John for nearly three years, so he might have held the Islands for part of that time. When Peter did return to the Plantagenet side in the summer of 1207, the King had not forgotten his forfeiture of the Islands. Letters of protection were issued to Peter permitting him to visit John's court in early August 1207, when the King would restore to Peter his land in England, and offer forgiveness 'over the Islands', as he had been advised to do by Ranulf III, Earl of Chester, and Ingeram de Préaux (Peter's brother).[6]

1205–6: the first reconquest

An important source for the first Plantagenet campaign of re-conquest is a work of literature in the French vernacular, the 'Romance of Eustace the Monk'.[7] This was written around the middle of the thirteenth century, probably in the Low Countries, of which the eponymous hero was a native. Being a work of lit-erature, the 'Romance' as a source for political history is problematical, but some of the material in the 'Romance' can be corroborated, and dated, from other sources.

Eustace was the younger son of an aristocratic family of the Boulonnais. The 'Romance' emphasizes his bravery in battle, his cunning, ingenuity and even magical powers, and his skills as a mariner. Independent evidence for the real Eustace's career con-firms that he was ambitious and self-serving, and also that he was indeed recognized as an exceptionally skilled seaman. According to the 'Romance', Eustace's alliance with King John had its origins when Eustace fell out with his lord, the Count of Boulogne, and was obliged to flee the Capetian realm. He offered his services to the rival Plantagenet king, probably early in 1205. King John employed Eustace on an expedition to the Channel Islands, equipped with thirty galleys. The Channel Islands were then under Capetian control, with a castellan named Romerel leading the inhabitants in resisting Eustace's landing. The 'Romance' naturally gives Eustace the leading role in the battle which followed, in which the Plantagenet invading force was victorious, expelling the Capetians and plundering and destroying property. Despite the heroics and wanton destruction described by the 'Romance', this was not a privateering expedition; it was in fact sanctioned and equipped by King John. A royal writ issued in November 1205 refers to money seized by Eustace the Monk and 'the justiciar's men', which they had rendered to the proper authority in England, William of Wrotham, Warden of the Sea-ports.[8]

The first attempt at reconquest of the Channel Islands can be dated to sometime in 1205. By 19 September that year, King John believed that his men had taken charge of Jersey, Guernsey and Alderney, and issued orders to parties unknown (their names are omitted from the record) to protect these islands, to maintain the peace and not to cause any damage.[9] The entry of this document in the official record was cancelled, however, so it is probable that it was never sent. Apart from this apparently premature royal missive, there are no records of Plantagenet government for the Channel Islands until the middle of 1206.

A second attempt at reconquest was made in the spring of 1206. This campaign was documented in the records of government, so that in contrast with the evidence for Eustace the Monk's campaign, we have dates and more reliable figures as well. Before the end of April 1206, a fleet of five galleys and three 'great ships' with 275 mariners crossed to the Channel Islands to serve the king for forty days.[10] This short campaign succeeded in establishing Plantagenet control. In May 1206, King John addressed a writ to Geoffrey de Lucy, Hasculf de Subligny 'and his faithful men in the Islands', ordering them to return some of the galleys and arrange for the recruitment of mariners and the supply of ships for John's planned campaign to Poitou.[11] Evidently Lucy and Subligny were now in control of the Islands. Before the beginning of July, the King had sent a consignment of flour to Geoffrey de Lucy in Guernsey. This may be evidence that the violence of the past two years had damaged crops, grain-stores and/or mills to the point of famine, or alternatively it may simply indicate that Geoffrey de Lucy's household and the Plantagenet garrison created an extra demand for flour which could not be met at short notice from local supplies without causing hardship and hence resentment.

Eustace the Monk does not appear again in connection with the administration of Jersey and Guernsey, but at some point he established a base on the island of Sark. This probably originated with a grant by King John, as discussed below, but Eustace finally lost the King's favour. In 1214, Plantagenet forces raided Sark and took possession of the island for the Crown. In the raid, Eustace's brother and uncle, their servants and men-at-arms were captured and taken as prisoners to Porchester Castle, but Eustace remained at liberty.

1216–17: the second conquest

The testimony of 1309 referred to two conquests of the Channel Islands by King John. It has been suggested that both occurred in the period between 1204 and 1206, with the fortunes of war swinging quite rapidly between the Capetians and the Plantagenets. The evidence for this period is, however, conclusive only in establishing that the Plantagenets emerged victorious by May 1206. In fact, the second Capetian conquest, and Plantagenet reconquest, occurred some ten years later, as part of the invasion of England by Prince Louis of France in 1216. Eustace the Monk was once again involved but this time on the Capetian side.

After the raid on Sark in 1214, if not before, Eustace had switched allegiance and, having eluded capture by the Plantagenets, continued his maritime activities. According to the near-contemporary English chronicle of Roger of Wendover, when the papal legate Cardinal Gualo Bicchieri asked Philip Augustus for a safe-conduct to travel to England in 1216, the French king warned him that if he should fall into the hands of Eustace the Monk and his associates 'who keep the sea-ways', the King would not be responsible for his fate. Eustace's activities were not only piratical, however. In May 1216 he was in charge of mustering a fleet at Calais – six hundred ships and eighty cogs, according to Roger of Wendover – to transport Prince Louis and his army to England, and in August 1217 Eustace again commanded the fleet attempting to deliver reinforcements to Prince Louis in London.[12]

The annals of Dunstable priory record that it was Eustace the Monk, 'pyratas fortissimus', and Geoffrey de Lucy who captured the Channel Islands on behalf of Prince Louis.[13] This is confirmed by the peace treaty that ended Prince Louis' campaign, which required the brothers of Eustace the Monk to surrender 'the Islands' to the new English king, Henry III.[14] The fall of the Channel Islands again, and the role of Eustace, is plausible in the light of the barons' revolt and the death of King John, as a result of which Philip de Aubigné, then Warden of the Islands, was pre-occupied with events in England, where he was one of the champions of the beleaguered Plantagenet regime. As Roger of Wendover noted, Eustace the Monk and other men serving Prince Louis controlled the English Channel at this time. Controlling the Channel Islands would have been an important part of Eustace's strategy, as well as revenge for his recent ejection from Sark.

The Dunstable annalist's identification of Geoffrey de Lucy as Eustace's accomplice is also plausible. Geoffrey was an important and influential royal servant; Roger of Wendover listed him among the 'evil counsellors' of King John in 1211, along with Geoffrey fitz Peter the justiciar, Peter des Roches, Bishop of Winchester, and William of Wrotham, Warden of the Sea-ports.[15] Geoffrey also had relevant experience. In serving King John he had specialized in the defence of the south coast of England and the Channel Islands; from mid-1206 to mid-1207 he was the king's representative in Guernsey. But around September 1215 Geoffrey joined the rebel barons. The many and various estates he held across southern England were promptly seized by the Crown. Soon after, he is recorded in episcopal records attacking the Hampshire estates of the Bishop of Winchester. Geoffrey may have been with Prince Louis to the end, since he was reconciled with Henry III on 19 September 1217, the day before the sealing of the Treaty of Lambeth, which ended Prince Louis' English campaign.[16]

The records of government add further weight to the evidence for a second Capetian conquest in 1216. The last record of Philip de Aubigné acting as Warden before the death of King John dates from 6 October 1215. There is then an interval, with no records of Plantagenet government in the Islands until the end of August 1217. During this period, a charter issued on 19 May 1216 by the increasingly desperate King John to Peter de Préaux's younger brother and heir, William, displays uncertainty as to whether the Channel Islands were under the King's control at all. John offered William de Préaux the forfeited lands of two of the rebels in England, but if he could not guarantee his possession of these, the King could choose to render to William 'the islands of Jersey' instead, for the service due from the Islands (in the days of Peter de Préaux the service due was three knights), or land in England worth £300, in which case William would render for the land in England the same service he would have rendered if he had possessed the Islands.[17] It looks as though John was not confident that he could make good a grant of either the lands of the rebels in England or the Channel Islands. Furthermore, the proposed grant of the Islands to William de Préaux would have required the removal of Philip de Aubigné from office as the king's representative in the Islands, unless, as seems likely, Philip had already ceased to hold that office due to the hostilities.

For most of the year 1217 Philip de Aubigné was in fact preoccupied with the defence of the south coast of England, especially vulnerable with the loss of the Channel Islands and Eustace the Monk's apparent control of the seaways. King John had died the previous year and a snapshot of the dire straits of his successor Henry III's regime and Philip's role in saving it comes from a report delivered by Philip on 27 February to the regency council, safe at Dorking, about the urgent need for military reinforcements at Rye.[18] By mid-August, Henry III's men had regained control of the south coast, but also had intelligence that reinforcements for Prince Louis had been mustered and were waiting to cross from Calais in a large fleet under the command of Eustace the Monk. Philip de Aubigné had command of the defenders, including the sailors of the Cinque Ports. On 25 August Philip and his men put to sea and engaged the French fleet in a sea battle off Sandwich (plate 13). The Plantagenet victory that day proved decisive, not least in that Eustace the Monk was captured and executed without delay.

With the loss of any hope of reinforcements, Prince Louis capitulated. A peace treaty was negotiated near London and sealed at Lambeth on 20 September. One of the terms of the treaty dealt with the Channel Islands. It required Prince Louis to send letters to the brothers of Eustace the Monk, ordering them to render the Islands to Henry III. If they failed to do so, Prince Louis would seize their lands and fiefs (in the Boulonnais) which were within his lordship. If they still refused to hand over the Islands, they were to be regarded as outside the terms of the peace treaty.[19] It appears that Eustace the Monk had held the Channel Islands, with his brothers as his lieutenants, until his death.

The sanctions against Eustace's surviving brothers prescribed by the Treaty of Lambeth do not seem to have been imposed in the event. The records of government indicate that Philip de Aubigné was restored as the representative of Plantagenet authority in the Channel Islands even before the treaty was sealed. A royal mandate issued at Sandwich on 28 August 1217 ordered that none should impede 'La Contesse' or another ship hastening from Portsmouth to Jersey carrying Philip de Aubigné's men on the King's business. A mandate dated 23 September ordered Philip (presumably by a deputy) to restore land in Jersey to Thomas the Dane.

The anarchic conditions of the end of John's reign had apparently made it possible for Eustace the Monk and Geoffrey de Lucy to invade the Plantagenet outpost of the Channel Islands in 1216 and to subvert what remained of the royal administration there in the name of Prince Louis. The Treaty of Lambeth provides a certain date for the Plantagenet recovery. This second Plantagenet reconquest in September 1217 explains the timing of the important mandate issued by Henry III's regency council to Philip de Aubigné on 13 February 1218, in which the right of the Islanders to be ruled according to the customs prevailing in the reigns of King John and his predecessors is formulated by the royal chancery for the first time.[20] If King John had reconquered and only just held on to the Channel Islands from 1206 to 1216, the reconquest of 1217 heralded a new regime under the regents of the young Henry III.

Securing the reconquests

To make good the reconquest of the Channel Islands, the Plantagenet regime took a number of new and forceful measures to secure its position in Jersey. These were *ad hoc* responses to the immediate danger from France, but had the effect of establishing the foundations of stable Plantagenet rule for the remainder of the thirteenth century. They included the building of Mont Orgueil castle and maintaining control of the seaways, and we will discuss these below. Equally important were measures that addressed the internal security of the island through sanctions against those suspected of harbouring Capetian sympathies.

Internal security

In response to various threats and crises from 1206 into the 1220s the Plantagenet regime imposed a variety of sanctions aimed at ensuring the loyalty of the people of Jersey. It was important that the population should not offer support to the Capetians, whether actively or passively. The sanctions were imposed both on property and on persons. They included the taking of the sons and other family members of tenants as hostages, the threat of seizure of the land of tenants who remained absent in France for too long, and the expulsion from the island of those residents suspected of disloyalty.

The demand to give hostages was probably made in 1206, as soon as Plantagenet authority was restored. The earliest reference to the hostages is February 1208, in a mandate ordering Richard de Carteret to keep in safe custody his nephew Philip, who was a hostage for Reginald de Carteret, Richard's brother. The taking of hostages was the only sanction John had against those Jersey landholders, the vast majority, who did not possess any land in England that could be seized if they betrayed the Plantagenet cause.

The hostages were taken to England and there distributed amongst a large number of custodians. This spread the expense of their maintenance and also had the strategic advantage of preventing any concerted action to liberate them by force. The royal mandates ordering the release of the hostages are a valuable early source for the names of Channel Island families, but unfortunately many of the hostages are identified only by their Christian names. For instance, the hostages held by the courtier Engelard de Cigogné are named only as John and Ralph, and those in the custody of the Sheriff of Northampton as Henry, Richard and William. Of a total of twenty-five hostages named in various mandates, only ten can be identified with particular families: Philip de Carteret, Colin Petit ('Parvus'), William Malet (the son of Robert Malet, who would die before William's return), Colin Norman, Ralph le Gallichan, Robert Hurman, Reginald 'Gunewar', Gervase Beket (described as a hostage for Richard Beket of Jersey), Robert de la Roche and John de la Croix.

The most important of the hostages was Philip, the son and heir of Reginald de Carteret. Reginald's loyalty to the Plantagenet cause must have been in question after 1204: although he had aided in organizing the defence of the Islands in 1203, he also possessed land in Normandy. Reginald's decision to sacrifice his Norman land and retain his land in Jersey was out of the ordinary, and there must have been uncertainty as to which course he would take. He regained King John's trust at least to some extent because in February 1208 the custody of his son was given to his own younger brother, Richard, then Constable of Winchester Castle. A few months later, Reginald received letters of protection from the King, copies of which were sent to the royal officials in Jersey and Guernsey, presumably so that Reginald could return to the Islands and recover his possessions there. Young Philip was still not freed, however. At some point he was transferred to the custody of a trustworthy royal servant, Stephen of Thornham. In November 1212, Stephen was ordered to deliver Philip from royal custody to Philip de Aubigné, who had recently been appointed as the king's representative in Jersey. This probably meant the end of Philip's stay as a hostage in England, since he is not named in the mandates ordering the release of the other hostages two years later, and was almost certainly connected with the betrothal of Philip de Carteret to Philip de Aubigné's niece, Margeria. A marriage alliance between the Carteret family and the chief Plantagenet officer in the Channel Islands was a sure sign of Reginald de Carteret's present and future good faith.

On 2 November 1214, King John wrote to the knights and worthy men of Jersey and Guernsey, thanking them for their good service and notifying them of the return of their hostages. Between that date and January 1215 the King sent a series of mandates addressed to those who had custody of the hostages, informing them that because of the fidelity and good service of his worthy men of Jersey and Guernsey, the hostages should be freed and permitted to return to their own parts.[21] The timing of this was probably connected with John's urgent need for friends and allies as the barons' rebellion got underway. The second Capetian conquest of the Islands in 1216 nevertheless proved that this was a misjudgment.

Further measures designed to ensure that the landholders of Jersey were loyal to the Plantagenet regime were introduced soon after the second reconquest. With tenants-in-chief who possessed land in Normandy as well as in the Islands it was relatively simple to determine which side they were on after 1204. If they had given their allegiance to Philip Augustus, they would have publicly acknowledged the fact, for instance by rendering homage, supplying military service or paying financial demands. Different considerations applied to the landholders whose only, or principal, tenements were in the Islands. They would not be called upon to render homage to Philip Augustus for their tenements because Capetian authority did not extend to the Channel Islands. But they were intimately connected with communities on the Norman mainland through marriage and other family relationships, patronage of the Church and trade. How could anyone, and most relevantly, the royal officials, know whether such individuals harboured Capetian sympathies? If suspected, what action could or should be taken to protect the Plantagenet regime from them?

A possible indication of Capetian sympathies was spending periods of time on the mainland, fraternizing with the enemy, but it was impossible and undesirable to prohibit all such contact. The Islanders depended upon travel to the mainland for trade, to buy necessary provisions and to attend to family business. This dilemma is reflected in a royal mandate, issued in February 1223, to the effect that if any of 'the knights of our islands of Jersey and Guernsey' should remain away on the mainland for more than eight days, the Warden was authorized to take his lands into the king's hands immediately and keep them until further order from the king.[22] Eight days was presumably reckoned sufficient for an innocent trip to the mainland. The time limitation would have prevented the traveller from journeying far beyond Lower Normandy, for instance to the Capetian royal court. In view of the specific application of this mandate to knights or warriors ('milites'), it may have been particularly aimed at preventing them from performing military service for the Capetians, in anticipation of Prince Louis' invasion of Poitou in 1223.

An earlier measure, of wider application to the Jersey community, was an inquest conducted by Philip de Aubigné, probably between 1217 and 1219, to ascertain which tenants were loyal and which were not. The royal mandate is no longer extant, but some evidence of the proceedings comes from a letter written to the King by some concerned citizens of Jersey or Guernsey.[23] Soon after Philip de Aubigné re-established Plantagenet authority in 1217, the regency council ordered him to 'take the assizes' in the Islands, apparently with a specific mandate to determine which of the tenants-in-chief were 'faithful or unfaithful' ('fideles aut infideles'). This was done by inquest, a routine procedure of convening a jury to answer specific questions such as this. The tenants-in-chief were already present, as they were obliged to attend the royal court when it was convened by the Warden to take the assizes. Once the juries gave their verdicts, those who were found to be 'infideles' were forced to abjure the island, in fear of their lives, leaving their land and chattels as forfeit to be taken into the king's hand. The letter had in fact been written to complain that too many of these 'infideles' had since received royal pardons and that their return to the Islands posed a threat to security and law and order.

The undated letter is corroborated by a series of letters from Henry III to the Warden of Jersey, between 1234 and 1236, issued for the benefit of individuals who had suffered in these proceedings. Typical is the case of Geoffrey Hugun. Henry III's letter narrates that Philip de Aubigné had presided over an inquest in which a jury was chosen to state 'who were faithful and who were unfaithful'. The jury enquired into the reputation ('fama et conversatione') of Geoffrey Hugun of Jersey. Their verdict was that Geoffrey was 'unfaithful' and had committed larceny. Geoffrey immediately fled to a church for sanctuary and by night took to a small boat and left the island. He then made a personal petition to the King and offered to place himself upon the verdict of a jury of twenty-four honest and lawful men from the three neighbouring townships in respect of the alleged crime. The King agreed and by this letter, dated 10 September 1234, ordered the Warden of Jersey to empanel the jury, 'according to the customs of the said Island', and if their verdict was that Geoffrey was 'rather more faithful than unfaithful' and that the accusation of crime was false, then the Warden should make peace with Geoffrey and restore his property.

Geoffrey Hugun was evidently only one of a considerable number of Jersey tenants judged to be 'unfaithful' in the same proceedings. Similar royal letters were issued for the benefit of nine others, including two women, each of whom had been condemned as 'unfaithful', obliged to take sanctuary in the nearest church in fear of death, and then abjure the island. At least one of the petitioners finally succeeded; in January 1236, Henry III restored to Stephen le Mercier his lands which had been taken into the king's hand. Another, Robert 'Frowelin', had a harder time of it. In his absence, the Crown had sold Robert's land, in the parish of St Lawrence, to Geoffrey le Buver. Geoffrey claimed in the royal court that he had purchased Robert's land in good faith some fifteen years after Robert's flight. Robert subsequently followed the same procedure as the other petitioners: he placed himself on the verdict of a jury of twenty-four local men and succeeded in clearing his name. Geoffrey then petitioned the King to be allowed to keep the land he had bought, rather than Robert recovering it from the hand of the King's official.

The names of ten individuals caught up in the inquests of Philip de Aubigné have survived in the records of government. These men and women were obliged to leave all their property and go into exile from Jersey, apparently under threat of capital punishment. No doubt there were many more; the documentary record as it survives is probably incomplete. Some would have accepted forfeiture of their lands in Jersey and chosen not to appeal; others perhaps wished to appeal but lacked the means to do so. The effect of these proceedings at the time must have been dramatic. One can imagine the atmosphere of a witch-hunt, with false accusations flying and perhaps used for political ends, to settle old scores between neighbours.

The procedure of accusation of 'infidelity' by a jury of eight men was subsequently used *ad hoc* in cases where an individual was suspected of having gone over to the Capetians, in particular, it seems when they were absent. For instance, Richard de Gray, Warden in 1226, conducted this procedure in respect of a

Guernsey tenant, Richard de 'La Ruwe', who was judged 'infidelis' while he was absent on business 'in Francia'.

Mont Orgueil castle

One very conspicuous measure taken by King John to secure his hold on the islands was the building of castles. Both Castle Cornet in Guernsey and Mont Orgueil castle in Jersey appear to have been founded at the same time, in a campaign of fortification undertaken upon the reconquest of 1206. The military function of the castles was important, of course, but it was not their only purpose. Mont Orgueil castle immediately became the focal point for the Plantagenet administration of Jersey, both materially and symbolically. The stone towers, perhaps whitewashed and with flags flying, perched high above the sea on a solid rock, broadcast the reality and permanence of Plantagenet authority to both the Islanders and the French (plates 16, 17).

The effect of Mont Orgueil must have been even more impressive considering that there do not appear to have been any castles in Jersey before 1204, at least not of the Norman motte-and-bailey type. Neither would one expect to find any. Prehistoric hillforts such as those at Câtel de Lecq and the promontory at Gorey would have provided some protection for the inhabitants against attack, but this threat diminished once the Cotentin came under the control of the dukes of Normandy in the early eleventh century. On the coast at St Helier, an enclosure defended by a substantial bank of stone and turf, dating from the ninth and tenth centuries, was replaced in the more peaceful conditions of the eleventh century by a farmstead and, in the late twelfth century, by the substantial dwelling-house described in the previous chapter (see p. 58).[24]

The phenomenon of castle-building that occurred in France in the eleventh and twelfth centuries, as counts and dukes struggled to exercise authority over recalcitrant castellans, was absent from the Channel Islands since none of the estates there were sufficiently large to support a military aristocracy. Similarly, there was no need for the frontier castles of increasing military sophistication which were constructed by the Marcher lords of Wales and northern England, and by the Plantagenet and Capetian kings on their frontiers during the late twelfth century. The Channel Islands were not on a frontier; on the contrary, they were securely situated within the Plantagenet empire. Sworn testimony in 1248 in which it was declared that there were no castles in the Islands before the reign of King John appears to be worthy of credence.[25] In the thirteenth century, references to Mont Orgueil in records of royal government often allude simply to 'the king's castle in Jersey': evidently there could be no confusion, as there was only one castle.

Some fortifications must have been constructed, or reinforced, in 1202–3, because there was a garrison of Plantagenet men-at-arms in the Islands; they must have had secure positions to defend. The apparent lack of permanent fortifications would have greatly assisted the Capetians in taking control of the Islands in 1204, if any resistance was offered at that time. Did the Capetians build the first castles? The 'Romance of Eustace the Monk' refers to the commander of the Capetian force in the Islands as a 'castellan', and boasts that after Eustace's triumphant pillaging of the Islands, 'there was nothing left to burn either in castle or manor', but this literary work should not be taken too literally as a source for architectural history.[26] The positions of Mont Orgueil and Castle Cornet in any event would not have been well-placed to defend against attacks from the direction of the south coast of England or from Brittany, so if the Capetians did construct any fortifications in the short time they controlled the Islands, they would not necessarily have been on the same sites as the present castles.

On recovering control of Jersey, King John's men cannot have taken long to choose the promontory at the northern end of the bay of Grouville as the site for a castle on this newly created frontier. Mont Orgueil is of course splendidly positioned to defend against attack from the east, from the Cotentin coast. The hill overlooking the castle was just too distant to be employed as a platform for siege engines by any attackers who might have gained a foothold in the island. The high, rocky promontory, rising steeply above the best natural harbour in Jersey, was invulnerable before the use of gunpowder. It was also apparently a parcel of royal/ducal domain, so the King's men would have a free hand in developing the castle and harbour. Philip de Aubigné is said to have dispossessed several tenants, including the prior of St Helier, of twelve acres of land in the vicinity of Mont Orgueil because cultivation of this land was deemed by him to be to the detriment of the castle.[27] In 1226, Hugh de Saint-Philibert was responsible for works on 'Jersey castle'. According to the account Hugh rendered to the Crown, he paid for setting out walls, improving wells, and making and repairing ditches, and he also purchased eight acres of land 'in front of the castle gate', presumably buying out the tenants.[28]

The first documentary reference to Mont Orgueil occurs in letters of King John dated 14 November 1212, giving notice that the King has committed to Philip de Aubigné the island of Jersey 'with the custody of our castle'.[29] The castle must have been in existence in some form by that date. In January 1226, five cartloads of lead were despatched from England 'for the works of the castles' of Jersey and Guernsey. If this was for the roofs, it suggests that some buildings were substantially completed. As the account of Hugh de Saint-Philibert indicates, there was still much to be done in 1226, especially around the perimeter.

The archaeological evidence is consistent with the oldest visible structures in the castle dating from the early thirteenth century. This earliest phase of construction saw the building of a two-storey keep and flanking towers on the ridge which forms the highest point of the promontory (plate 17). A stone curtain wall enclosed the area, landward of the keep, now known as the Middle Ward. The curtain walls of both the Middle Ward and the Lower Ward beyond, with mural towers and gatehouses, are probably nearly contemporary.

The layout and the scale of these structures were determined by the contours of the rock. The keep is relatively small and thin-walled, perhaps because of the narrowness of the ridge, but its eminent position exaggerates its height and renders it invulnerable to attack.

The keep comprises a vaulted undercroft and a first-floor hall. There may originally have been an upper storey or wall-walk above the hall. The undercroft below is floored with the jagged, bare rocks of the promontory (plate 18). Although identified in the past as a chapel, or the crypt of a chapel above, this area was almost certainly designed for storage, with exterior access from a door at ground level, and internal access to the first-floor hall by a stair in the north-east corner. The main entrance to the hall above was a wide, round-arched door approached by external stairs on the western (inland) side. This was a well-proportioned and well-lit space (plate 20). The present ceiling, with its assymetrical pointed barrel-vault, is not an original feature. A pair of windows on each of the long east and west walls were large and deeply splayed with round-headed arches. There was no need for narrow arrow-loops: the castle rose so high above a steep cliff on the seaward side that attack from that direction was evidently not contemplated. On the seaward side the external wall of the keep serves as the curtain wall of the castle. From the first-floor hall there was direct access to the flanking towers to north and south (plate 19). These were similarly two-storeyed and, with up-to-the-minute internal latrines, may have served for accommodation as well as defence.

Within the Middle Ward would have been structures to house the many and varied functions carried out in a thirteenth-century castle. There is documentary evidence for a chapel, pantry, bakehouse and prison; the medieval well survives. There must also have been a kitchen, stables, storerooms and accommodation for the garrison and servants, and a strongroom for storing large amounts of coins and other valuables. In addition, there was probably a range of lodgings on a more lavish scale than was available in the keep for the accommodation of important residents and visitors.

The castles were constructed as fortifications, for defence against invasion from France. In a letter to Henry III, Philip de Aubigné described with satisfaction a visit to the Channel Islands on one occasion when military tension was high. At Guernsey 'we found your men of the castle and the people armed and excited against your enemies and theirs, so that ... they [would not] suffer us to enter the limits of the port until they had seen our standard unfurl'. De Aubigné further reported that he found both of the King's castles, presumably Castle Cornet and Mont Orgueil, secure and equipped with knights, sergeants-at-arms and victuals.[30]

But the castles also functioned as the headquarters of the Plantagenet administration. The Exchequer at Caen was no longer available as a seat of ducal authority for accounting for the financial administration of the Islands, nor could the ducal treasury be stored in Norman castles. Although we know something of the administration of Jersey before 1204, as discussed in Chapter Two, there is no evidence for the locations or venues at which the administration was carried out. This is partially explained by the fact that the administration was then on such a small, local scale that it did not require any specialized or permanent structures: the 'curia' or hall of the neighbour who then held office, or some communal meeting-place such as the parish church, would have sufficed. After 1204, the changed circumstances required a centralized administration for the whole island.

The evidence for the thirteenth century is fragmentary, but it is probable that the royal administration of Jersey was conducted at Mont Orgueil from soon after 1206. The castle's most obvious function was as a secure place for the treasury; we know that the proceeds of the hearth-tax, collected every three years, were deposited here. Rents due from the tenants of royal domain were paid at the castle on certain days each year; around 1300, Ralph Lemprière customarily paid the rent due for his land in the parish of St Helier at the castle on 'the feast of St Paul' (30 June).[31] This suggests that the castle was more than a place to store treasure; some accounting took place there too. In an inquest in 1254, sworn testimony was given that the abbot of Mont Saint-Michel was accustomed to receive 4 *l.*10 *s. tournois* each year as royal alms, in three payments of 30 *s.*, by the hand of the Warden or his deputy, 'in the castle of the lord king in the island of Jersey'. The three instalments may represent regular terms when payments or accounts of the royal revenues were rendered.[32] The king's Receiver, an office in existence before 1299, could disburse as well as receive funds and was evidently based at Mont Orgueil.

The castle was also used as a prison. In the Middle Ages, imprisonment was not a sentence following conviction, rather it was a stage in legal process. Malefactors were arrested and locked up only until sureties could be found for their appearance in court. Around 1300, William Ranulf of the parish of St Peter spent some time imprisoned in the castle after having been apprehended for taking rabbits from the king's warren. In 1299, Simon le Coueror brought an action in the royal court, claiming that William Galbard had procured his imprisonment in the castle such that Simon could not secure his own release until he agreed to give William some land in the parish of Grouville.[33] Rather surprisingly, there is no evidence that the royal court was held in the castle, and the sessions of the royal justices in 1299 were held in St Helier. An account of the Warden in 1329 refers to repairs to the roof of 'the house in which pleas of the king are held', which might have been within the castle.[34]

Mont Orgueil castle, as it would later be known, thus rapidly developed as not only the defensive stronghold of Jersey against attack from Normandy, but also as the headquarters of the royal administration.

Naval supremacy

Control of the seaways was an important factor in the success of the Plantagenets in regaining and keeping control of the Channel Islands. It may explain why Philip Augustus did not attempt to reinvade after the demise of Eustace the Monk in 1217. The Capetians were accustomed to mobilizing armies and fighting on land, not least because until the late twelfth century the lands under Capetian control, centred on the Ile-de-France, were land-locked, with only a single North Sea port at Montreuil-sur-Mer. In contrast, the Plantagenets were accustomed to travel by sea, initially from the need for crossing between England and Normandy after 1066, then from 1154, sailing further afield between the British Isles and Aquitaine as well. An English contingent on the Second Crusade travelled by sea to reach the Mediterranean, and Richard I sent most of his crusading army by this route in 1190. The experience of existing in a political entity that was linked by waterways – the navigable rivers of England, the English Channel, the Irish Sea and the great rivers of western France – made the Anglo-Normans experts at shipping not only human passengers and their horses, but also treasure and heavy cargoes, like stone from Caen to England, and the lead shipped from England to Jersey and Guernsey for castle roofs.

In the conquest of Normandy and the Loire Valley, the Capetians had the advantage that all of their resources – men, horses, arms, provisions – could be mobilized by land, with comparatively short journeys to the frontier from the compact Capetian royal principality, consisting of the Paris basin and parts of Flanders, or from allied Brittany. In contrast, for the Plantagenets to be able to employ the resources available from the British Isles to reinforce the Normans and Poitevins, everything had to go by sea. No matter how expert the mariners, this was a serious logistical disadvantage. The difference between the Plantagenet and Capetian positions became even more marked in Plantagenet campaigns of reconquest launched (literally) after 1204. It was not sufficient to muster an army; the Plantagenet kings also had to muster a fleet for transport and suffer the vagaries of weather and tides before they had even reached the theatre of war.

The situation of the Channel Islands was unique in this regard. Invasion and conquest of the Islands necessarily involved a naval expedition, whether by Capetians or Plantagenets. Here, the Capetians lacked the logistical advantage they enjoyed on the French mainland. The fact that the distance by sea was much less between the Islands and France, compared with England, was no particular advantage either. The same size of fleet was required whether the sea journey was ten kilometres or 110. All other things being equal, in conquering and defending the Channel Islands, the advantage lay with the Plantagenets, with their greater experience and expertise in sea-faring.

The importance of shipping is demonstrated in the English records of government concerning the Channel Islands in the aftermath of 1204. One of the very earliest records after the reconquest of Jersey and Guernsey indicates the new role of the Islands in the organization of shipping in the Plantagenet dominions. A mandate issued by King John on 19 May 1206, addressed to Geoffrey de Lucy and Hasculf de Subligny and the king's other faithful men in the Islands, ordered them immediately to despatch, with two galleys, a knight and a clerk who would be able to speak knowledgeably and enthusiastically with steersmen and sailors, on the sea route from La Rochelle to Saint-Mathieu de Finistère or wherever else they could be found, to persuade them to join the king's service without delay. The knight and the clerk were also charged to record all the places where they found boats, the names of their steersmen and their cargoes. When the knight and the clerk had completed this assignment, they were to return to the Islands and submit their report to Geoffrey de Lucy and Hasculf

de Subligny, who were ordered to send it on to William of
Wrotham immediately. In the meantime, Geoffrey and Hasculf
were also ordered to send to Portsmouth, as soon as possible, the
boat of Alan the Young of Shoreham and any others that they had
in their possession.[35]

Other royal orders regarding expenditure on shipping of men
and materials account for much of the evidence we have for Plantagenet government of the Islands in this period. For instance, on
15 April 1207 King John ordered the officials of Portsmouth to
supply a ship for Thomas Painel, Hasculf Painel and Hasculf de
Subligny to cross to Guernsey, the cost of which would be borne
by the Crown provided each swore that he would not take anyone
with him who was not of his own household; the Crown was not
in the business of providing free trips to the Channel Islands. On
one occasion between September 1208 and September 1209,
three galleys were sent to Jersey, carrying certain knights, twelve
horse-sergeants, and ten foot-sergeants and their provisions, all
covered with canvas awnings, and an additional ship was hired to
carry the horses.[36]

The evidence for all this maritime activity on behalf of the
royal government is admittedly biased in favour of the Plantagenets, because we lack similar records of government from
France. No doubt there was a certain amount of shipping on
Capetian royal business, but the simple geography of the Capetian
dominions suggests that this was less important than it was to the
Plantagenets, who were trying to retain control of Ireland, Wales
and Aquitaine as well as the Channel Islands.

The chronicler Roger of Wendover vividly describes English
naval supremacy in his account of the battle off the coast of
Kent in late August 1217, a narrative retold by Matthew Paris and

illustrated by him in his 'Chronica Majora' (plate 13). The campaign of Prince Louis to take the English crown was faltering, and he was now confined to London and the south-east. Louis' wife Blanche of Castille (King John's own niece, who had designs on the English crown) had recruited reinforcements in northern France to go to her husband's aid. The fleet assembled to transport the reinforcements on 24 August was not anticipating a battle. They did not know that the Plantagenets had gained control of the south coast of England and were in fact watching for the expected French fleet. The French were reluctantly, and disastrously, forced to engage in naval combat when the English ships attacked from the rear.

> When the French discovered this, they flew to their arms and made a bold resistance... Philip de Aubigné with his crossbow men and archers sending their missiles amongst the French soon caused great slaughter amongst those who opposed them. They had moreover galleys peaked with iron, with which they pierced the ships of their adversaries and sank many of them in an instant; they also threw hot lime-dust on the sea, which, being borne by the wind, blinded the eyes of the French. A severe engagement took place between the fleets, but that of the French, who were not skilled in naval warfare, was soon defeated; for the crews were struck down by the weapons and arrows of the English sailors, who were used to naval fights, pierced them with their javelins and arrows, or cut them down with swords and lances, whilst others bored holes in their ships' bottoms and sank them.[37]

The impressive display of naval tactics by the Plantagenet fleet had a significant result for the Channel Islands. The Capetian fleet was under the command of Eustace the Monk, and in defeat,

Eustace was captured and executed. Whichever side he purported to serve, Eustace had been a menace to the stability of Plantagenet rule in the Channel Islands. At last he was no more, and the Capetians had no one to take his place.

Administration from 1206 to 1216

Immediately prior to 1204, there was no royal administration in Jersey because the island was held in fief by Peter de Préaux. Once Plantagenet control was restored in 1206 it was necessary to establish a new regime. Furthermore, the circumstances were now different from before 1200, when the Islands were first granted to Peter de Préaux. Royal government of the Channel Islands then had been a branch of the administration of the Cotentin, involving financial accounting at the Exchequer at Caen and regular visits by royal justices from Normandy, but now that was impossible. The priority was the restoration of law and order, and defence against the Capetians. Arrangements were made *ad hoc* to address the immediate priorities, but new and permanent institutions were also introduced in this period.

The energetic administration of the Islands between 1206 and 1216 is demonstrated by the earliest version of the so-called 'Constitutions of King John' dating from *c.* 1248.[38] This text will be discussed in more detail in Chapter Six, but here it will be argued that it preserves a number of mandates issued by King John concerning the Channel Islands. The 'constitutions' deal with a variety of legal, military and commercial matters. The first two 'constitutions' concern the legal system, but only as to procedural matters rather than substantive law. Their purpose was the preservation of law and order, and ensuring that the Islanders would continue to have access to royal justice. The remaining

six 'constitutions' are a combination of fiscal and security measures, with an emphasis on trade and commerce. The following
summary will indicate their tenor. King John ordered that there
should be keepers of the ports of the Islands, who would keep the
ports well and not allow any harm to occur to the king's interests.
He ordered that any 'foreign' ship, that is, one not under the Plantagenet king's authority, which landed in the Islands, should be
charged one marc of silver. Similarly King John ordered that all
small boats carrying fish from the Islands to Normandy should be
charged 3 *solidi*. The salting of congers was limited to the period
between Michaelmas and Easter and the revenues put out to farm
by the royal officials, the same as for fish-drying (*éperquerie*). All
merchants should pay customs on their wares, but the men of the
Islands were exempt in respect of their own provisions. The final
'constitution' is now only partially legible; it deals with fishermen,
prescribing three days each week in which they could perform a
particular activity (perhaps go to sea, or sell their catch).

The 'Constitutions of King John' are evidence of the King's
concern for the well-being of the Islanders, including their access
to justice, their financial burdens, and the organization of the
lucrative fish-drying industry.

Royal government was delegated to some of King John's most
trusted and able men, capable of both civil and military administration. These were sent to the Islands to do whatever needed to
be done to keep them under Plantagenet control, and at the same
time to exercise royal authority in collecting revenues and administering justice. Royal mandates regarding their sea-crossings
demonstrate that the early Wardens did visit the Islands, but they
were probably not normally resident, since they had other duties
and commissions to perform in the king's service.

From 1206 until 1212 Jersey, Guernsey and Sark were administered separately, each with its appurtenant islands and rocks. In
Sark there was apparently no ducal/royal domain, and therefore
no royal administration, before 1203.[39] The island had been held
throughout the twelfth century by the Vernon lords of Néhou,
until it was forfeited by Richard de Vernon in 1203. This power
vacuum attracted Eustace the Monk, who occupied the island
with a party of his relations and countrymen. It is possible that
King John originally granted Sark to Eustace, either to administer
for the Crown or as a fief, so that his possession of the island was
quite legitimate. King John gave Eustace land in Norfolk and
Somerset (according to the records of royal government), and also
enabled him to build his own palace in London (according to the
'Romance'); why not Sark as well? In late October 1214, Plantagenet forces raided Sark, apparently under the authority of Peter
des Roches, Bishop of Winchester, chief justiciar and regent. We
do not know whether this action was the cause of Eustace going
over to the Capetian side at around this time, or the result. In
December 1214, after King John's return from Poitou, Peter des
Roches was ordered to deliver possession of Sark to the Warden of
the Islands, Philip de Aubigné. Thereafter, Sark was administered
with Jersey and Guernsey under the Warden of the Islands.

In 1206, King John appointed Hasculf de Subligny to govern
Jersey and Geoffrey de Lucy to govern Guernsey. There is some
logic to this disposition. Hasculf's Continental estates were situated
in the hinterland of the Bay of Mont Saint-Michel, in north-
eastern Brittany and the Avranchin, and Jersey is the island closest
to these. As will be seen below, for a generation after 1204 there
was a strong connection between custody of Jersey, or all of the
Channel Islands, and the aristocracy of north-eastern Brittany.

Geoffrey de Lucy had no apparent connections with Normandy or Brittany, but his landholding and official activities were concentrated in the south-east and the south coast of England, to which Guernsey is somewhat closer and more accessible by sea. In 1207, however, Geoffrey was replaced by Philip de Aubigné.

Hasculf de Subligny had custody of Jersey for a longer period, from 1206 to 1212. He was perhaps a 'safe pair of hands', a mature man with a family tradition of royal service and also experience of baronial lordship. Since *c.* 1175, Hasculf had been lord of the honour of Combourg, in north-eastern Brittany, by right of his wife, Isolde de Dol, a marriage made possible by the patronage of Henry II towards Hasculf's father, the loyal courtier John de Subligny. Hasculf also inherited land near Caen and in Somerset and Cornwall. In view of the sea route between Saint-Malo and the south-west of England, Hasculf was one of the few Anglo-Norman barons who might have visited Jersey before 1204. He initially chose the Capetian allegiance in 1204, but returned to King John's service in March 1206. Hasculf's son, John de Dol, who succeeded him as lord of Combourg at this date, recorded in one of his charters that his father had fled to England on account of the wrath of the French king.[40]

Hasculf de Subligny is first mentioned in the records of royal government in May 1206, when he and Geoffrey de Lucy had recently taken up their respective posts. These records provide evidence of Hasculf's visits to Jersey and some of his responsibilities as the king's representative on the island. Hasculf must have returned to England, because he crossed the Channel from Portsmouth in April 1207. In October, he was ordered to give a fief in Jersey to Thomas Painel, for which Thomas had already rendered homage to King John. Another royal writ ordered Hasculf to ensure the Norman abbey of Bellozanne had possession of its land in Jersey, since the abbot had come to terms with the King. In February 1208, Hasculf crossed the Channel again, this time from Southampton direct to Jersey, with Thomas Painel and others travelling to the island on royal business. Hasculf must have had with him the writ, dated 27 February, ordering him to give the land of Silvester de Furnet in Jersey to Silvester's brother Ingeram. From a writ of March 1208, addressed to the king's 'baillivi' of the islands of Guernsey, Jersey and other islands, and therefore including Hasculf de Subligny, it appears that Hasculf was responsible for taking into the king's hand the churches and other possessions of Norman monasteries in Jersey.[41] At this point, there is an unfortunate lacuna in the records until 1212, but the character and the pattern of Hasculf's activities are reasonably clear.

Hasculf can be credited with two other achievements of more general significance while governing Jersey. First, some twenty years later, in 1230, it was said that Hasculf had reduced the customs exacted from the men of Jersey for taking food and other things of lesser value out of the island, presumably to sell at market.[42] This measure may perhaps be identified with one of the 'constitutions' of King John. Second, Hasculf must have overseen the foundation of Mont Orgueil castle. We have argued above that there were no castles in Jersey before 1204, but in 1212, when Hasculf's appointment ended, he was ordered to deliver 'the island of Jersey and its castle' to his successor.

Hasculf handed over custody of Jersey to Philip de Aubigné, who would play a much greater role in the history of the Channel Islands, and indeed of the English realm. The ancestry of Philip de Aubigné is highly relevant. Like Hasculf, Philip's kin enjoyed the patronage of the Norman kings of England and also possessed a barony in north-eastern Brittany.[43] As lord of Combourg, Hasculf had dealings with both William, lord of the Breton barony of Aubigné, and Philip's elder brother, Ralph de Aubigné, who was lord, by marriage, of the barony of Landal; both were near neighbours of Combourg. The brothers Ralph and Philip de Aubigné must also have had a close relationship. As noted above, Philip cemented an alliance with the Carteret family by the marriage of his niece, possibly Ralph's daughter; and Ralph's son, also named Philip, became Philip's heir. Hasculf de Subligny and Philip de Aubigné, as well as Philip's brothers Ralph and Oliver (later Philip's deputy in Jersey), were part of the same community of aristocrats of north-eastern Brittany who had tenurial interests in England.

As a younger son, Philip had to seek his own fortune. He first appears in the 1190s in the entourage of the Anglo-Norman magnate Robert, Earl of Leicester, but thereafter he became an important and trusted servant of King John. In August 1207, early in his career, Philip was given custody of Guernsey and 'the other islands which Geoffrey de Lucy had'[44]. A royal writ dated 14 November 1212, ordering Hasculf de Subligny to hand over Jersey, informs him that Philip de Aubigné has been given custody for as long as it pleases the King.[45]

From November 1212, Philip had custody of Jersey and Guernsey together (and Sark from December 1214). In January 1214, Oliver de Aubigné was 'in the king's service' in Jersey, no doubt acting as his brother's deputy there. For the next two years or so, the role of Philip, or his deputies, was the same as Hasculf's had been – executing royal orders to maintain the King's rights in the islands and to ensure that where the King offered patronage or reward, the beneficiary actually received his due. For example,

Philip was ordered to restore to the abbey of Mont Saint-Michel its land and possessions within his bailiwick. He was also ordered to give to Thomas the Dane the land in Jersey he held of Baldwin Wake, which was then held in wardship by William Briwerre.

A royal writ dated 8 June 1213 records that a boat carrying pilgrims from the Channel Islands landed at Portsmouth and was sent back, at the expense of the royal treasury, in the custody of Philip de Aubigné's servant, Nicholas, because Philip had requested it. More ominous was his request in the autumn of 1214 for three galleys, which he could retain around the islands for as long as he needed them. The Capetian threat intensified after July 1214, when the Plantagenets were decisively beaten at the battle of Bouvines. Despite the worsening situation for King John's regime, both in the Channel Islands and in England, Philip and his deputies continued to administer the Islands until the second Capetian conquest in 1216.

As Wardens of Jersey and Guernsey under King John, Hasculf de Subligny and Philip de Aubigné were able administrators, both in civil and military matters, but some further explanation is required of their common background of royal patronage and close ties with Brittany. Surely relevant is the dream of reuniting the Plantagenet lands. Until the mid-1220s, the Plantagenet kings believed Normandy could be regained. Henry III still held most of Poitou at the time. The duchy of Brittany was not securely attached to the Capetian regime because of the self-serving politics of the dukes of Brittany, Guy de Thouars and Pierre de Dreux, regent and spouse, respectively, of Alice, the heiress of the duchy. The Channel Islands, after 1204, were the vital link between England, Brittany and the remaining Continental possessions. Men whose heritage was on the Continent, in Brittany and Lower

Normandy, as well as in Britain, were ideally qualified to act in the interests of preserving what remained of the 'Plantagenet empire', in a way that men whose interests lay only in England were not.

The involvement of Geoffrey de Lucy in Guernsey, and later as Warden of the Islands, points to an additional factor – the role of the bishop of Winchester. Geoffrey was in many respects a worthy successor to his grandfather, Richard de Lucy 'the Loyal', Henry II's justiciar. His great misfortune, and the misfortune of the Lucy estate in England, which came to be divided amongst Richard's granddaughters, was to be illegitimate. Without the prospect of an inheritance, Geoffrey made his way by the patronage of his uncle, Godfrey de Lucy, Bishop of Winchester. Godfrey died in 1204 but as a result of his patronage Geoffrey was established as a figure of importance in Hampshire and the south coast.

Naturally the bishop of Winchester exercised considerable authority in this region, both as head of the church and as a major landholder. This role was greatly augmented during the episcopacy of Peter des Roches. Peter was a royal clerk from the Plantagenet heartland of the Touraine, related to William des Roches, the Seneschal of Anjou. He was rewarded with the bishopric of Winchester and succeeded Godfrey de Lucy in 1205. Thereafter, Peter was one of the most important royal counsellors, chief justiciar and regent in 1214, a loyal supporter of King John during the rebellion, and guardian of Henry III from 1216. As an Angevin, Peter was naturally inclined to favour the recovery of the Continental territories of the 'Plantagenet empire', and this policy would have given him an interest in the Channel Islands. Peter des Roches may even have had some direct responsibility for the government of the Islands. As noted above, when Eustace the Monk's men were ejected from Sark, the bishop at first took the island into his own hands. Peter des Roches certainly played a role in the exercise of Plantagenet authority in the Channel Islands, but probably in his capacity of chief justiciar rather than as bishop.

Peter des Roches was also one of the 'aliens', the Frenchmen who were serving the Plantagenet ruler in England and the remaining Plantagenet domains overseas. These men had sacrificed their lands on the Continent and followed King John into exile in England. Maintaining their loyalty, and their desire to follow the King in his campaigns to regain their lost estates, with judicious grants of lands and offices, was a delicate business. They were an alien minority amongst the Anglo-Norman aristocracy, most of whom had ceased to have tenurial interests beyond the British Isles a generation or more ago. Peter des Roches has been identified as a patron of this faction.[46] The appointments of Hasculf de Subligny and Philip de Aubigné may have been his doing. Hugh de Saint-Philibert, a close associate of Geoffrey de Lucy and Warden of Jersey in 1226, was a tenant of the bishop of Winchester in Overton (Hampshire). Similarly, Eustace de Greinville, a Norman who was one of Peter des Roches's household knights, was rewarded with land in Jersey between 1204 and 1218. In 1221, when Philip de Aubigné delegated his custody of the Channel Islands to his nephew Philip, it was with the authority of Peter des Roches. By this time, de Aubigné and des Roches were close associates, having collaborated in the custody and tutelage of Henry III since 1216. Philip could even be found hunting on the bishop's estates.[47]

The personnel and policies of the Plantagenet regime in the Channel Islands may have been determined, or at least influenced, by Peter des Roches, but there was another influence at work – the place of the Channel Islands in the region of the Western

English Channel. When political relations with the nearest adjacent part of this region, the Cotentin, were severed, the other shores came to the fore. The men appointed to represent Plantagenet government after 1204 were not randomly chosen from all regions of England and Normandy. Their tenurial, dynastic and political interests were concentrated in the lands on the northern and southern shores of the Western English Channel – the West Country and the south coast of England and north-eastern Brittany.

King John, who had been Lord of Ireland, the West Country, the Channel Islands and the honour of Mortain before 1199, was well equipped to appreciate the strategic importance of these shores in controlling a unique corridor for shipping from the British Isles and Ireland. After the loss of Normandy (and Brittany), the Plantagenet monopoly of this seaway was nearly lost; indeed it *was* lost to Eustace the Monk for a time in 1216–17. It became vital to retain possession of the Islands, and after 1204, they became part of a co-ordinated strategy of defending the seaway of the Western English Channel from both its northern and southern reaches.

This co-ordination was most important during times of military crisis, as can be seen from the careers of Geoffrey de Lucy and Philip de Aubigné. One of the earliest records of Geoffrey is as Warden of the Sea-ports of Sussex, in February 1205, when he was ordered not to allow any ship to leave port without royal licence. This was not a desk-job; Geoffrey was active in the king's service at sea, including the campaign to reconquer the Channel Islands. While he was later in rebellion (see p. 88), Philip de Aubigné took charge of the defence of the south coast, but as soon as possible in 1217 Philip was returned to the Channel Islands. After his reconciliation with Henry III and, with the King planning a campaign to invade Poitou, on 29 August 1224 Geoffrey de Lucy was appointed Warden of the Sea-coasts ('custos maritima') with the barons of the Cinque Ports. A few weeks later, on 8 October 1224, Henry III granted Geoffrey the islands of Jersey and Guernsey and the other islands of the king which were then in the custody of Philip de Aubigné junior.[48] This appointment restored control of both sides of the Channel to one experienced naval commander for the duration of hostilities with France, ending – for the time being – in May 1226.

CHAPTER FOUR
Land and people

A CENTURY AFTER the events of 1204, some Jersey tenants-in-chief were summoned before the royal justices to show by what authority they claimed certain rights which ought to have been the prerogative of the King. These included the right to take wreck of the sea on the shores of their lands, the right to possess a warren, the right to try felons and keep their chattels as forfeit, and the right of *éperquerie* (the seigneurial monopoly on fish-drying). Those who appeared at the assizes of 1309 to defend their claims were Peter de Samarès, Philip de Carteret, William le Gallichan, John de Carteret and Lucy his wife, and Philip Levesque. All claimed their entitlement to these rights on the grounds that they had them of old and that their ancestors had them from time immemorial. The King's attorney argued to the contrary that, as in England, no one could enjoy these privileges without special warrant from the King. In particular, the Crown argued that all these 'natives' ('indigene') had their status in the island from the time of the last conquest of King John. The second Plantagenet reconquest of the Channel Islands occurred, as we believe, in 1217. This was not 'time immemorial', because legal memory was deemed to have begun with the accession of Richard I in 1189, so the tenants were obliged to show proof of royal warrant.[1] There ensued a legal dispute between the Islanders and the Crown which lasted for decades. These Jersey landholders claimed the right to exercise certain royal prerogatives on their own account, and they could be described as 'natives'. For them, 1204 was not a turning point in the history of the tenements they held, but the Crown took an opposing view. How could these two positions be reconciled?

We will argue that the 'natives' of 1309 represented families who had held land in Jersey since time immemorial, or at least since before 1189. What had changed in the aftermath of 1204, as the Crown indeed argued, was their status as landholders. In short, prior to 1204, these Jersey families had held their land as tenants of Norman aristocrats whose estates were principally on the mainland. Over a period of several decades from 1204, these Norman aristocrats forfeited or abandoned their Channel Island estates. The sitting tenants resident in Jersey thereby came to hold their lands directly of the Crown. Now in effect tenants-in-chief, they formed the new élite of Jersey society.

We will consider briefly the evidence for landholding in Jersey before 1204. It is not possible to be comprehensive, or even systematic, on the subject of tenure in Jersey either before or after 1204. No register or census of landholdings exists from this period for Jersey or for the Cotentin. Tenants of the Channel Islands are not included in the list of 'Normans' whose lands in England were forfeited in 1204. If such a list ever existed for the Channel Islands it is lost without trace. Some particular references occur in English records of government to the King's grant to one individual of land in Jersey forfeited by another for having taken the side of the Normans, and these will be discussed below. For the most part, however, we have only fragmentary or circumstantial evidence.

The history of the fief 'des Mouriers' in the parish of St John is typical, and this is one of the better documented cases. Before 1204, Richard de Ouville gave to the abbey of Saint-Sauveur-le-Vicomte the tithe of all his land known as 'des Mouriers'. He was apparently succeeded by William de Ouville, who had died by December 1214, when his widow Lucia was given her dower in Jersey by order of King John.[2] The fact that Lucia must have had difficulties gaining possession of her dower-lands could indicate that William had taken the Norman side before his death, but there were plenty of other causes for widows to have to sue for their dower in the thirteenth century. The principal evidence that William had forfeited his Jersey land comes from the Crown surveys, or 'extents', of 1274 and 1331. The 1274 extent records that the 'feodum de Morers' in the parish of St John includes the escheat of William 'de Dunvill, miles', and the 1331 extent helpfully if belatedly records that 'le fief Dorvile alias Le Mourier' is an 'old escheat of the Normans'.[3]

The major landholders in Jersey in the eleventh and twelfth centuries were not based in Jersey; the greater part of their estates were on the mainland. This was true not only of the tenants-in-chief, men who held their land directly of the dukes of Normandy, but also of many of *their* tenants, to whom they had given fiefs in Normandy and in Jersey. Even from the early eleventh century there is evidence of estates in the Cotentin which included parcels of lands and rights in the Channel Islands. These connections may have been of long standing. In *c.* 1025 Richard, Duke of Normandy, gave to the monks of Mont Saint-Michel all the lands in the district of Coutances that had belonged to the monastery of Saint Paternus (Saint-Pair) before it was destroyed by the Vikings, including the islands of Chausey.[4] In the mid-eleventh century, Adelelm, a retired ducal retainer, gave to Mont Saint-Michel various parcels of land and rights which belonged to his estate of La Croix in the Avranchin, including three ploughlands in Jersey. Similarly, when Reginald de Carteret first endowed Mont Saint-Michel with land in Jersey, no later than 1125, the land was described as 'the royal alms of St Germanus in Jersey', and was evidently connected with the church of Saint-

German de Carteret on the mainland, which Reginald gave at the same time.[5]

The two dominant dynasties of the Norman aristocracy with interests in Jersey before 1204 were the Vicomtes, lords of Saint-Sauveur-le-Vicomte, and the Vernons, lords of nearby Néhou. The Vicomte family is usually associated with Guernsey, because we have a specific record of the fact that Duke Richard II gave half of that island to Nigel, his deputy ('vicecomes') in the Cotentin, *c.* 1020. It appears that the Vicomtes also possessed a substantial portion of Jersey. Around 1090, Nigel II Vicomte issued a charter confirming all the possessions of the abbey of Saint-Sauveur-le-Vicomte, the monastery he had founded near his castle, including three Jersey churches, St Peter, St Clement and St Helier. There is no record of who gave these three churches to the abbey, but it could have been Nigel himself. He had already given the six parish churches in his half of Guernsey to his church of Saint-Sauveur, the future abbey. However, Nigel later rebelled against the young Duke William II, was exiled for some years from 1047 and his estates were forfeited. Duke William took the opportunity to give the six parish churches of the 'fief du Cotentin' in Guernsey to the priory at Héauville, which the dukes had founded for the distant but influential abbey of Marmoutier at Tours. When Nigel II was pardoned and his estates restored, he could not eject the monks of Marmoutier, and instead he compensated the canons of Saint-Sauveur for their loss. It may be that this was the occasion when three parish churches in Jersey were donated to the future abbey of Saint-Sauveur. A fourth parish church given to the same abbey was certainly in the lordship of the Vicomtes. Between 1100 and 1130, Roger de Sottevast gave the parish church of St Brelade, with the tithe of the parish ('villa'), to the abbey of Saint-Sauveur-

le-Vicomte, with the seigneurial consent of Nigel III Vicomte.[6]
Soon afterwards the dynasty came to an end in the male line when
Roger Vicomte died fighting for King Stephen in Normandy. The
barony passed to Roger's daughter Leticia and her husband, Jordan
Taisson, and their descendants. Leticia inherited her forebears' role
as patron of Marmoutier's churches in Guernsey, but there is no
further evidence of the family as seigneurs in Jersey.

The Vernon family were the seigneurs of a barony in the
Cotentin which took its name from the castle of Néhou. The
barony included the islands of Alderney and Sark, and also large
estates in Jersey, in the northern parishes of St Ouen, St John and
St Martin le Vieux. Some or all of this had been given as fiefs to the
Vernons' Cotentin tenants, such as the families of Barneville and
Vauville. In the first half of the twelfth century, the land used by
the Vauville family to found the priory of Bonnenuit in the parish
of St John was land they held of William de Vernon, who gave his
consent to the transaction.

The fact that several names of Jersey fiefs, as recorded in the
thirteenth century, are derived from the toponymics of other
Vernon tenants from the vicinity of Néhou suggests that these
constituted the Jersey lands of the barony of Néhou which had
been parcelled out as fiefs to those tenants. These are the fiefs of
Anneville (possibly in the parish of St Martin le Vieux), Morville
and Orglandes (both in the parish of St Ouen). All three families
were associated with the household of the Vernon family of
Néhou and of its English branch (from 1100), the Redvers earls
of Devon. Roger de Orglandes attested a charter of William de
Vernon concerning tolls levied at Barneville, while Peter de Orglandes was a clerk of Richard de Redvers (*c.* 1100–1107). Ralph de
Anneville was steward of the honour of Carisbrooke (the Redvers

lands in the Isle of Wight) in 1190 and Herbert de Morville was Richard de Vernon's steward of Sark in 1196.[7]

Other Cotentin families held land in Jersey of one or more seigneurs. The Sottevast family was a cadet branch of the Magneville, tenants of the Vernon lords of Néhou. Before 1170, Eudo de Sottevast held land in the parish of St John as a tenant of the Vauville seigneurs and thus ultimately of the Vernons.[8] When it came to Channel Island landholding, the Sottevasts had other seigneurs as well. In Guernsey, they held the 'fief Sotuas' of the earl of Chester's 'fief le Comte', and in Jersey they held a substantial tenement in the parish of St Brelade, including the parish church, as tenants of the Vicomtes de Saint-Sauveur. In the thirteenth century, Adam de Sottevast was a tenant-in-chief of land in the parish of St Lawrence but finally forfeited his lands in Jersey sometime before 1274 when he chose the French allegiance.[9]

Other Cotentin families who held land in Jersey, either as tenants-in-chief or as tenants of other (as yet unidentified) Norman seigneurs, included those with the following toponymics: Barneville (seigneurs of the fief of Jerbourg in Guernsey, and tenants in Crapoudoit and elsewhere in Jersey), Buisson of Glatigny (Grouville), Carteret (St Ouen), 'Furnet' (Rozel; their place of origin in Normandy is unidentified), Gonneville (William Suen de Gonneville held land in the parish of St John of the fief of Roger Wake),[10] Le Hommet (St Clement), Ouville (St Peter and St John), Salinelles (the future Samarès manor in St Clement), 'Scrakkevilla' (St Mary; 'Scrakkevilla' was in the parish of Heugueville-sur-Sienne) and Surville (St Helier), and also the Norman family names Malet (Grouville) and Pinel (St Peter). Unfortunately almost nothing is known of the history of these families or their fiefs before 1204.

The aftermath of 1204 brought about a tenurial revolution in Jersey, but it was not simply as a result of forfeitures by the Norman aristocrats. The process was more complicated than the 'high profile' records of forfeitures and grants to royal favourites imply. There were forfeitures, and some new men, royal favourites, benefited from some of them, but the most important result of the forfeitures was to elevate the status of the under-tenants to that of tenants-in-chief. In contrast to the forfeitures, some Norman seigneurs were loyal to the Plantagenets and kept their Jersey lands at the expense of their Norman estates, notably the Carterets. Then there was a third category of response, perhaps the most common but also the least disruptive and hence the most incon-spicuous in the records. Many families anticipated the risk of forfeiture and arranged their affairs so that their landholdings in Normandy and the Channel Islands were divided and distributed amongst different branches of the family. Since the Jersey tene-ments were normally the less valuable, they tended to be allocated to younger sons or to daughters, thereby creating new Jersey-based branches of these Norman families.

In general, the subject of the forfeiture of land in England or Normandy by the Anglo-Norman aristocracy, as they adhered to one party or the other after 1204, is one that has attracted relatively little detailed study.[11] Recent studies of particular families have demonstrated that cross-Channel landholding in fact continued for several decades.[12] The evidence for landholding in Jersey is entirely in keeping with this conclusion. Individuals were natu-rally motivated to try to hold on to as much land as they possibly could, but in more general terms the survival of cross-Channel estates is consistent with the policy prevailing at the Plantagenet court for nearly fifty years after 1204, that England and Normandy should be reunited under Plantagenet rule. As a matter of principle, it was desirable to conserve the pre-1204 *status quo* as far as possible in order to facilitate the hoped-for reunion.

It follows from this that not all forfeitures occurred in 1204. In the assizes held in Jersey in 1309, it was asserted for the Crown that 'the Lord King John after his second conquest in these Islands as also in England banished and disinherited all the Normans living in France or Normandy as well ecclesiastics as laymen, and disposed of their lands and goods at his will'.[13] Nevertheless, it appears that in the decades that followed 1204, individual tenements were forfeited as 'land of the Normans' ('terra Normannorum') as and when the Crown saw fit. In some cases it seems that a sitting tenant was permitted to retain land in Normandy and in Jersey for as long as he lived, but when it came to succession to his land, the heir would not be permitted to continue this arrangement, which was perhaps based on a personal relationship of trust between the tenant and the Plantagenet authorities.

The forfeiture of estates as 'terra Normannorum', which were awarded to new 'foreign' tenants-in-chief, is apt to take undue prominence in the historical record simply because these transactions were recorded by the royal chancery. In contrast, estates remaining in the hands of the same tenants or families after 1204 would not have given rise to such enduring written records. We will begin with the forfeitures, and then discuss their new possessors, before moving on to the evidence for continuity of tenure in Jersey after 1204.

In fact only two individuals can be identified as having forfeited their lands in the immediate aftermath of 1204. These were Thomas du Hommet, who held the 'fief du Hommet' in the parish of St Clement for the service of one knight,[14] and Silvester de Furnet, lord of Rozel. The two men were acquainted before 1204; Silvester attested a charter of Thomas du Hommet concerning a gift of wheat from Jersey to the nuns of Holy Trinity, Caen.[15] The 'fief du Hommet' is first recorded as being in escheat in October 1207, when it was regranted to Thomas Painel as a hereditary fief for one knight's service.[16] The land of Silvester de Furnet in Jersey was in escheat by February 1208, the date when King John awarded it to Silvester's brother, Ingeram, who was one of the King's household knights.[17]

There is no specific evidence that either forfeited his fief for having gone over to the Capetian side; the evidence is purely circumstantial. Land might fall into the king's hands for a variety of reasons, including the death of a tenant-in-chief. Without some reference to the land being in escheat as 'terra Normannorum', it is not safe to assume any sinister cause. The case for Thomas du Hommet's infidelity is somewhat stronger, in that he was a younger son of the Constable of Normandy, who went over to the Capetians in 1204, and the regranting of his escheated land to a man who had lost his land in Normandy is typical of the fate of 'terra Normannorum'. Silvester de Furnet possessed land in the *vicomté* of Bonneville on the mainland before 1204 and therefore may have chosen the Capetian side, but from the terms of King John's grant of his lands to his brother, it is equally possible that Silvester had recently died, leaving his brother as his heir.[18]

The extent of Jersey of 1274 contains several references to tenements forfeited because their tenants adhered to the Norman cause. These cannot all be proved to date from 1204, although some may have. They include the fiefs of Anneville, of William de Henot (or Henaud), Morville, Orglandes and Ouville, and lands belonging to William Pinel and Adam de Sottevast, and the families of Surville and Vauville. In the case of William Pinel, records of the royal chancery confirm that his land in Jersey was escheated as 'terra Normannorum' and awarded to William de Cheney, but not until 1244. William Pinel's estates on the Norman mainland probably exceeded his Jersey lands in value, so his defection some time after 1204 was predictable. It seems that William's land was forfeited before 1244, but was retained in the king's hand. The material date was William's death, which occurred shortly before April 1244, when an inquisition *post mortem* found that William's heirs were his two daughters, both of whom were married and in the allegiance of the King of France.[19] Presumably, while William lived, Henry III hoped he would return to the Plantagenet allegiance and reserved his land for him.

The Vauville family is one whose fortunes on the mainland and in Jersey can be traced in rough outline. The family had acquired an estate at Vauville by 1066, when William de Vauville participated in the Norman Conquest and was for a time Constable of Exeter Castle. He had previously joined Duke William II in endowing the collegiate church of St Mary in the duke's castle of Cherbourg with the church of Alderney and land in that island. In the early twelfth century, William de Vauville's descendants possessed substantial estates in Vauville and its environs, including houses in the thriving ports of Barneville and Cherbourg. In Jersey, they possessed the church of St John and other land in the parish, some of which they used to endow the priory of Bonnenuit. Most, if not all, of these estates, including those in Jersey, were held of the Vernon seigneurs of Néhou. Richard de Vernon has the distinction of being one of the first Norman barons to give his allegiance to Philip Augustus, not waiting for the Capetian invasion of 1204. There is no record as to whether Richard II de Vauville, or his son

William, followed his lord then, but the Vauville 'fief' in Jersey must have been forfeited at some time. Thomas, a younger son of Richard II de Vauville, became vicar of the parish church of St Mary in 1208, but there is no further evidence of any secular possessions of the family in the Channel Islands thereafter. In contrast, the family thrived in Normandy. William, the eldest son of Richard II, was lord of Vauville in 1217. Some circumstantial evidence comes from the records of the priory of Le Mont Saint-Michel at Vauville, founded for Cerisy abbey by Richard I de Vauville in the mid-twelfth century. At a date unfortunately unrecorded, Richard II set out terms for re-establishing the priory's finances.[20] Their original endowment had included a tenth of whatever the Vauville household possessed in food, drink, candles and other necessaries, for the monks' maintenance. For reasons which are not explained in this document, the monks' takings had diminished and new arrangements were made for them to receive the sort of livelihood the founder had intended. Although the original endowment included a mill in Jersey, which the priory apparently retained because of its status as tenure in alms, the new arrangements do not mention any estates in Jersey as sources of income. One might speculate that this transaction was prompted by the loss of the Vauvilles' Channel Island lands, which would have substantially reduced their revenues, in cash and in kind.

Some forfeitures certainly occurred later than 1204. Whatever uncertainties surround the 'escheats' of the 'fief du Hommet' and of Rozel in 1206–7, both were later forfeited as 'terre Normannorum' by the very same men to whom they had been awarded by King John. Some time around December 1212, when Thomas Painel acquired royal confirmation of his possession of the land of

Thomas du Hommet as a hereditary fief, the Anglo-Norman
magnate Enjuger de Bohun stood as surety for Painel's fidelity and
for his undertaking that he would not solicit any other land in
exchange for his lost land in Normandy other than the land of
Thomas du Hommet in Jersey.[21] Painel did not keep his word,
however: between 1214 and 1217 he went over to the French side
and forfeited the 'fief du Hommet'. Ingeram de Furnet also
changed sides and forfeited Rozel sometime between 1226 and
1231.

The beneficiaries of the forfeitures may be divided into two
categories. First, there were Norman seigneurs who had chosen
the Plantagenet side and lost their patrimony in Normandy. They
deserved some compensation for this sacrifice, and lands forfeited
by those who had gone the opposite way were an obvious choice.
But in principle both John and Henry III hoped that they would
be able to restore the Norman lands, so they granted the 'compen-
satory' estates only on an interim basis, until the reconquest of
Normandy. The formula adopted by the royal chancery was, 'until
our land of England and the land of Normandy will be
together'.[22] Presumably the intention was that the Jersey estates
would then revert to the Crown. The relatively few Anglo-
Normans who received land in Jersey as compensation were not
intended to keep it for posterity, rather they were men who were
supposed to be keen to recover their own patrimonial land in
Normandy.

The second category were courtiers and household knights
who needed to be paid. As Henry III's finances became strained,
grants of escheated lands to sustain them in royal service were
increasingly resorted to, in England as well as in Jersey. This may
have had strategic benefits, placing at least some of the island

tenements in the hands of loyal warriors, but equally it may just have been a matter of the availability of estates to use for patronage. A further consideration is that the men who received land in Jersey from Henry III all served the King 'in parts overseas', in Gascony and Brittany and elsewhere. Since their duties regularly involved sea journeys between the Plantagenet dominions, estates in the Channel Islands would have been rather convenient. These grants could be made expressly to sustain the grantee 'while he was in the king's service', but could become life interests or even be made hereditary.

One such grantee was Eustace de Greinville, a cadet of the family of Grainville-la-Teinturière (Seine-Maritime), who made a successful career as a household knight of Peter des Roches, Bishop of Winchester and sometime regent of England. It is unlikely that Eustace inherited his land in Jersey since his family were based in Upper Normandy; he probably acquired it after 1204 through the patronage of Peter des Roches. It was during the regency, in January 1218, that Eustace received royal confirmation of his right to hold certain land in Jersey. Before he in turn forfeited, Eustace was able to transfer his Jersey land to his English kinsman Gilbert de Greinville.[23]

The evidence for Eustace de Greinville's tenure as the beneficiary of land forfeited by Norman seigneurs is only circumstantial. Otherwise, there are just two clear examples of Jersey lands forfeited as 'terre Normannorum' being used to maintain royal servants as grants for their life, or period of service, only, and there are similarities between the two cases. These involve William de Commendas and Aimery Buche.

William de Commendas is first recorded in royal service in the 1225 campaign in Gascony. He was a Poitevin and a knight of the royal household. In November 1232 William was sent to 'parts beyond sea' on the king's business, in company with Drogo de Barentin, and he fought in Henry III's Brittany campaign from 1233 to 1235. From 1236 (and probably before) to September 1240 William received a money-fief of £10 *per annum* from the King. At a date or dates unknown, the King awarded him in addition life-tenancies in the manor of 'Wykeham' (possibly Wickhambrook) in Suffolk and in the fief of Morville in Jersey. William possessed this fief until his death in 1240 or 1241.[24]

Aimery Buche was probably another Poitevin in the service of the Plantagenets.[25] By 1221 he was married and held land in Somerset and Dorset. In 1225 he joined Richard, brother of Henry III, on the Gascony campaign and in June 1227 was again sent to Gascony on the king's business. From 1227 (if not before) to 1238 Aimery received a money-fief of £10, payable at the Exchequer each year. On 24 April 1233, he received a grant of 'the land in Jersey which was Ingeram de Furnet's', 'to sustain himself in the king's service, for as long as it should please the king'.[26] In 1247, after Aimery's death, this was described as £10 worth of land 'in villa de Rossel' held by Aimery Buche 'of the king's bail' for his life.[27]

On the deaths of Aimery Buche and William de Commendas, Henry III was careful to take their lands in Jersey back into his own hands. Instead of retaining them, the King was keen to use them for patronage, and now took the different approach of granting them in hereditary tenure. In 1241, William de Cheney received the fief of Morville, and in 1247 Drogo de Barentin, then Warden of the Islands, received the fief of Rozel. Predictably, William de Cheney and Drogo de Barentin each founded a dynasty of important and influential tenants-in-chief. In official positions of authority and as wealthy seigneurs, their descendants would often come into conflict with the 'native' tenants.

The acquisitions of land in the Channel Islands by William de Cheney eclipse those of all other 'foreigners' and suggest that Cheney set out to concentrate his newly acquired wealth in the Channel Islands. He began with the advantage that Philip de Aubigné was his kinsman and patron. It may have been through this connection that William first acquired land in Jersey, as a tenant of Gilbert de Greinville, some time before 1239. When Gilbert de Greinville forfeited his estates, the land that William had acquired from Gilbert was not escheated but awarded to him by Henry III in hereditary tenure. In addition to the fief of Morville, William acquired from the Crown the land of William Pinel in Jersey, at first for his life (1244) and then in inheritance 'until the reunion of England and Normandy' (1253). William also acquired the island of Jethou, to hold of Mont Saint-Michel for his life, and substantial interests in Guernsey as well.

Incidences of forfeiture for taking the Norman side and the redistribution of the forfeited estates to royal favourites in the aftermath of 1204 are dramatic and comparatively well documented, but we would argue that they were in fact not the norm. First, because not all forfeited estates were redistributed; some were kept in the king's hands – Henry III, for example, did not let go of the fief du Hommet after its forfeiture by Thomas Painel. When fiefs were retained in the king's hand, only the seigneurial domain and revenues were administered by royal officials, and portions of these were redistributed as a matter of convenience or patronage. The immediate under-tenants, the vavassours, became tenants-in-chief for their shares of the fief, provided they did not themselves follow their lords and take the Norman side. By this process, families whose only, or principal, landholdings were in Jersey came to greater prominence than before.

Secondly, numerous individuals and families astutely took action to arrange their affairs so as to avoid forfeiture, or at least minimize their loss. These arrangements included the division of mainland and island estates between members of the same family, and the exchange of land with a third party. Indeed, some estates may already have developed in this way before 1204, with the Jersey lands in the hands of a cadet branch: the political separation of Normandy and England just made such divisions more formal and enduring. As ever, much of the evidence is circumstantial, simply the appearance in the documentary record of a Cotentin family in Jersey before 1204 and a tenant in Jersey with the same toponymic or family name after 1204. More information is provided in some cases by the records of legal disputes that arose decades afterwards.

This is illustrated by the history of the fief of 'Scrakkevilla' in the parish of St Mary. Richard de Scrakkevilla died probably not long before 1240, leaving property worth 10 *livres (tournois) per annum* in his fief in Jersey as well as land in Normandy.[28] Richard's son and heir seems to have chosen the Norman side. Presumably anticipating forfeiture of the Jersey land, the heir exchanged it with Margeria, the wife of Jordan de la Hougue, for some land of hers in Normandy. This transaction was completed with the consent of Drogo de Barentin, then Warden of the Islands (Jordan de la Hougue was his deputy), and Richard's heir then presumably left permanently for Normandy. When the Crown's rights in Jersey were surveyed in 1274, it was asserted that the 10 *livres'* worth of land in the fief of 'Scrakkevilla' now held by Margeria as a widow should be in the king's hand because it was forfeited as 'terra Normannorum'. In defence of her title, Margeria argued that Richard himself had been loyal to the kings of England all his life and had died seised of the land. An assize jury said the same thing, and Margeria was allowed her seisin 'until the King or his council order what ought to be done about it'.[29]

Less straightforward was the history of the fief of 'Robelins', also in the parish of St Mary, held in 1204 by Richard Levesque. Richard gave half of the fief to his daughter Gervasia, presumably as her dowry, but later (possibly at his death) the other half of the fief was forfeited because Richard took the Norman side. This did not prevent Gervasia from remaining in possession of her half, which she sold as a widow to a kinsman, Jordan Levesque. Jordan and Nicholas Levesque were both prominent in the administration of Jersey in the mid-thirteenth century, so the family was not tainted by Richard's defection.[30] It was not until the half-fief purchased from Gervasia had passed to Jordan's son, William, that the authorities under Otto de Grandison belatedly decided that this estate should be taken into the king's hands as an escheat on the grounds that Gervasia could not sell land that her father had forfeited.[31] It looks rather as though this was a late thirteenth-century attitude and not a representation of the state of law and society in Jersey before 1259.

A more straightforward, and successful, arrangement was made by Jordan de Barneville, who possessed estates in the Cotentin, in Jersey and in Guernsey (the fief of Jerbourg, the future Sausmarez). Jordan, now an old man, was still alive, and in Normandy, as late as December 1203 or 1204,[32] but there is no record of his estates in the Islands being forfeited. Jordan was succeeded by his four daughters, including Eleanor (probably the eldest) and Nicola, and divided his Channel Islands and mainland estates between them. Nicola received all of Jordan's estates in the Channel Islands. She was married to Maurice de Lucy, who died fighting for King John in the Islands, leaving their son and heir, Jordan, an infant. The record of a case in the Norman Exchequer in 1216 appears to refer to the inheritance of Jordan senior. In 1216, Eleanor de Barneville had recently died, leaving as her heiresses her three sisters, two of whom were 'in the peace' of Philip Augustus. The third sister was said to be 'in England' but the justices ordered her share of the inheritance should be reserved in case she should 'come to the king's peace'.[33] The 'English' sister must be Nicola. It appears that Jordan de Barneville anticipated the risk of forfeiture of his Channel Islands estates and gave the whole to Nicola either as her inheritance or as her dowry when she married. With a husband who was presumably related to Geoffrey de Lucy, Nicola would not forfeit the Channel Islands estates, but meanwhile Jordan and his other daughters could retain the (probably more extensive) Norman land.

Adam de Sottevast also seems to have tried to protect at least some of his Jersey property from forfeiture by using it as the dowry of a female relative. Before 1240, Adam gave a rent of 10 measures of wheat he held by hereditary right in the parish of St Lawrence with his niece Joanna in marriage to Ralph le Gallichan. Otherwise, Adam forfeited his lands in the fief of Handois in the parish of St Lawrence for taking the Norman side.[34]

Compared with those who changed sides, there remained a number of Jersey tenants who retained their land after 1204. The Salinelles, seigneurs of the manor of Samarès, may have forfeited their estates in Normandy; the Carterets certainly did. In 1230, Philip de Carteret announced his intention to go to the French king to ask for his land to be restored. He did not intend to stay in

Normandy – he assured Henry III that he would return home to Jersey on the completion of this business – but he wanted to use the land to marry off his daughters. If husbands were found for them in France, the young King Louis IX could not object, but there is no evidence that Philip met with any success in this venture.

Not all the tenants-in-chief before 1204 were Norman aristocrats. The family names of le Gallichan ('the Galician'), Lemprière ('the Emperor') and Vinchelez (Winchelsea) suggest their ancestors had settled in the Channel Islands from places outside Normandy, and therefore their Norman lands, if any, were unlikely to exceed the value of their estates in Jersey. Both le Gallichan and Lemprière appear in the 1180 Norman Exchequer roll as tenants in the 'ministerium' of 'Groceium', le Gallichan certainly as a tenant-in-chief. Vinchelez appears even earlier, in the mid-twelfth century, perhaps holding a fief of the Carteret seigneurs in the parish of St Ouen.

Families residing in Jersey and whose landholdings were relatively modest might have held little or no land in Normandy, and therefore did not have to make a choice as to their allegiance. Before 1204, these held their land in Jersey as tenants of seigneurs based in Normandy, or of the Crown. They are obscure to us because they made only a faint impression on the documentary records from before 1204. These would include the families Burnouf, Faledoit (a rare occurrence of a Jersey toponymic), Fondan, Goeis, Godel, Hastein, Horman, La Hague, La Hougue, Levesque, Malet, Norman and Petit. After the forfeitures of 'terre Normannorum', they found themselves effectively tenants-in-chief of the land they and their ancestors had always held as under-tenants. The sudden rise in their importance is epitomized by the fact that they were obliged to send hostages to England in 1206 (see p. 92). They also acquired new tenements, which had become available for redistribution by the Crown out of the forfeited 'terre Normannorum'. These families, along with le Gallichan, Lemprière and Vinchelez, appear in the thirteenth century as the elite of Jersey society, ranking only below the seigneurs of Carteret and Samarès in the social hierarchy. The importance of this development was not merely social, however. The change in the status of Jersey from an offshore branch of the administration of Normandy to a political entity that was virtually self-governing under Plantagenet supervision, gave this class of 'native' landholders new opportunities to participate in the government of the island at the highest level, as will be discussed in Chapter Six. Henceforth they could wield power and influence undreamt of by their forefathers. It is no wonder that they supported the Plantagenet regime.

CHAPTER FIVE
Jersey and the Norman Church

COMPARED with the momentous changes in lay society, the effects of the separation from Normandy on the church in Jersey were insignificant. In ecclesiastical and spiritual terms, there was no change and no tension because Jersey remained part of the diocese of Coutances. For all strictly religious purposes, such as the appointment of priests to the parish churches and priors to the priories, and in matters of liturgy, everything remained the same as before 1204. Conflict arose only at the interface of the ecclesiastical with secular authority, in relations of Church and State. Ecclesiastical authority over the Church in Jersey was now vested in an archbishop (of Rouen) and a bishop and abbots resident in Normandy who were the subjects, even the agents, of a foreign and hostile sovereign power, while secular authority was in the hands of the Plantagenet king of England.

In the immediate aftermath of 1204, once Plantagenet authority was restored, the Norman monasteries which possessed parish churches and other estates in Jersey were deemed to be aliens and enemies. At first, the abbots, the monks and their servants were not free to travel within the Plantagenet territories without first obtaining letters of protection from the royal chancery, no doubt at a price. When King John restored to the abbot of Bellozanne his land in Jersey it was strictly conditional upon the abbot giving security that neither he nor his men would cause any harm to the king or his land.[1] At the same time, it appears, the possessions of the Norman clergy in the Channel Islands were taken into the king's hand. In or shortly before October 1207, the abbot of Bellozanne successfully petitioned the King to restore 20 *livres'*

worth of land in Jersey which John himself had given to the abbey
before he became king. Evidently this land had been taken into
the king's hand between the Plantagenet reconquest in 1206 and
October 1207. Bellozanne did not possess a church in Jersey, only
land which was cultivated for the abbey's profit.

Churches were a different matter. In March 1208, the King's
officials in the Channel Islands received orders to give to Hasculf
Painel, an Anglo-Norman courtier, all the churches of the monks
in all the islands.[2] In effect, this meant that eleven out of the twelve
parish churches of Jersey were in the king's hand. The fate of the
twelfth, St Saviour, which belonged to the cathedral chapter of
Coutances, is uncertain. The mandate of March 1208 is not necessarily limited to parish churches either. The 'churches' then in the
king's hand could also have included the priory churches, all of
which were also possessed by Norman monasteries.

When it came to restoring the possessions of the Norman
monasteries in Jersey to their abbots, there was no single act
of restoration. One by one, it seems, the Norman abbots came to
terms with King John, and mostly within a relatively short time.
As noted above, the abbot of Bellozanne had his land restored
almost as soon as it was seized, but perhaps his case was special
in that no churches were involved, and the property had been
given by John himself. Already in 1208, the abbot of Cerisy
claimed the right to present a vicar to his two parish churches in
Jersey, St Mary and Grouville.[3] It was not until the end of November 1212 that Philip de Aubigné was ordered to restore the land
and possessions of the abbey of Mont Saint-Michel in his jurisdiction. The abbeys of Saint-Sauveur-le-Vicomte and Holy
Trinity, Caen, received gifts of property in Jersey from William
de Salinelles, lord of Samarès, in 1219 and 1221 respectively, so

they too must have regained control of at least their temporal possessions by then.

King John's policy towards the Jersey possessions of the cathedral chapters of Coutances and Avranches is not recorded. Peter des Roches, as Bishop of Winchester from 1205 to 1238, certainly took an active interest in the Islands. In 1309, the king's attorney before the royal justices claimed he was ready to prove that the Channel Islands were once part of the bishopric of Exeter.[4] But even if the Channel Islands had come under the spiritual authority of an English bishopric, whether Winchester or Exeter, it would not have prevented the Norman bishops from possessing estates in Jersey. The bishop of Avranches, for instance, retained possessions in England, at Porchester, Swanwick and Southwick in the diocese of Winchester, until the mid-thirteenth century.

The history of the possessions of the bishop of Avranches in Jersey is quite obscure, due to loss of the documentary evidence. In the thirteenth century, the bishop of Avranches received half of the tithes due to the Church in the parishes of Trinity and St Lawrence, and possessed lands and other rights in these parishes and in St John, the details of which are lost. In the assizes of 1309, the then bishop claimed they had been held 'since time immemorial'. The parish churches of Trinity and St Lawrence were in the hands of the dukes of Normandy in the twelfth century, so it is possible that these possessions derived from a ducal gift which could have dated from as early as the eleventh century. The bishops continued to enjoy the tithes and the revenues from their estates after 1204, but not without difficulty. Before 1249, the right to collect the tithe in the parish of Trinity had been farmed out to Ralph le Gallichan. The episcopal archives apparently once contained numerous records of the king of England ordering that what was due to the bishop of Avranches in tithes and rents should be duly rendered. The interests of the bishop of Avranches in Jersey are recorded by the place-name Ville à l'Evêque in Trinity and, indirectly, in Avranches manor (St Lawrence).

The experience of the possessions of the bishop of Coutances was different. The bishop possessed only a small estate in the parish of St Saviour, a sort of home-farm for the vicar of the parish church. The interest of the bishop of Coutances in Jersey, through the agency of the archdeacon of the Islands, was in exercising spiritual authority. The bishop was not so interested in temporal possessions, land and rights, as in possession of ecclesiastical authority over the whole island. Since this does not appear to have been seriously challenged in the aftermath of 1204, there is no evidence that the bishop's possessions were taken into the king's hands.

After the immediate seizure and then gradual restoration of the possessions of the Norman monasteries in Jersey, their history was the history of the other 'alien priories', the estates of French monasteries in England. Because these estates were held in perpetual alms, they were immune from being forfeited as 'terra Normannorum'. This did not prevent the king taking the 'alien priories' and their revenues into his own hand from time to time when political circumstances seemed to justify it. At times of open hostility with France, the monks were subject to restrictions on their activities, including travel, and prohibitions on their remitting money to the French mother-house. For most of the thirteenth century, however, the monks in Jersey did not suffer unduly at the hands of the Plantagenet regime.

The aftermath of 1204 may even have brought benefits to the Church in Jersey at the parish level. At some time in the first half of the thirteenth century the twelve parish churches all received new roofs. Their original thatched wooden roofs were replaced by pointed barrel vaults constructed from rubble stone. The precise date and the reason for this development are not known, but it has been suggested that it was a response to the conditions of insecurity after 1204.[5] The fighting over Jersey between Plantagenet and Capetian forces between 1204 and 1217 is certain to have involved the plunder and burning of buildings. According to the 'Romance of Eustace the Monk', after Eustace had recaptured the Channel Islands for King John, 'there was nothing left to burn either in castle or manor'.[6] While we cannot rely on this as an accurate report of conditions in Jersey in 1206, it does reflect the realities of campaigning in the early thirteenth century. The parish churches with their thatched roofs would have been vulnerable to destruction by burning and may well have suffered at this time. The provision of stone roofs protected the churches from the risk of fire in future, as well as improving their fabric. Who paid for this expensive building project? It could have been the Crown, anxious to mollify the Islanders. It may be relevant that the hall of Mont Orgueil castle received a new stone roof, with a pointed barrel vault, in the same period. The re-roofing programme could equally have been organized by the bishop of Coutances, to make good the injury to the interests of the various Norman monasteries and his own cathedral caused by damage to the parish churches.

The greatest source of conflict between the Norman Church and the Plantagenet regime in Jersey was over jurisdiction. This conflict was not strictly of the bishop's making, rather it stemmed from the anxiety of the Plantagenets that their sovereignty in their French dominions was vulnerable to the exercise of jurisdiction by the 'French' authorities. In Gascony, Plantagenet authority was undermined by the right of the Gascons to appeal for justice to the French royal court, the Parlement de Paris. In the Channel Islands, the Plantagenet regime did not have to contend with a rival secular jurisdiction; competition instead came from the 'French' court of the bishop of Coutances. This occurred when disputes arose which, by virtue of the parties or the subject matter involved, could be within the jurisdiction of the Church rather than secular courts. During the twelfth century there was a rapid growth in the jurisprudence of the Roman Catholic church (canon law) and a corresponding increase in the types of legal matters that were claimed by the Church as subject to the jurisdiction of ecclesiastical, rather than secular, courts. For instance, since fornication was a matter of sin, and marriage was a sacrament, Church courts had the exclusive jurisdiction to determine questions of the validity of marriage and the legitimacy of offspring. All members of the clergy, too, were entitled to invoke ecclesiastical jurisdiction even in disputes involving subject matter that was otherwise entirely secular.

Apart from appeal to the papal court, the ordinary ecclesiastical authority for Jersey was the bishop of Coutances. Cases under the jurisdiction of the Church were heard in the court of the bishop, normally at Coutances. In the thirteenth century, the competition for jurisdiction between secular and ecclesiastical courts was difficult enough when both operated under one lay ruler, as in England or France. When the secular court was that of the Plantagenet king of England, and the ecclesiastical court was that of a French bishop, there were real problems.

At least three different grievances about episcopal jurisdiction appear from the sources of the late thirteenth century. One was simply loss of revenue. Before the royal justices in Jersey in 1309, counsel for the Crown asserted that the king had lost 1000 *livres* (a suspiciously round number) in the proceeds of justice as a result of the loss of cases to the bishop's court.[7] A second was that clergy apprehended for crimes and handed over to the ecclesiastical authorities in Coutances were receiving favourable treatment, to the point that (as the Crown alleged) clerics based in the Channel Islands could do as they wished with no fear of reprisals or punishment.[8] This was presumably an affront to royal dignity, but also perhaps a problem for law and order in the Islands.

The third issue, the most relevant to the laity, was the problem of proceedings being commenced in the bishop's court at Coutances against lay men and women from Jersey. In due course the party would be summoned to appear, and then incur either the expense and inconvenience of travelling to Coutances, or the financial cost of having judgment entered against them in default of appearance. As so often in this story, the interests of the Islanders coincided with the interests of the Plantagenet regime. The defendants to suits brought in the ecclesiastical court complained about the time and expense involved in attending court in Coutances, compared with the privilege they enjoyed of not having to leave Jersey for any secular suits. The earliest instance we have found of a complaint about legal proceedings in the court of the bishop of Coutances dates from 1274, but no doubt the problem arose soon after 1204.

During the episcopacy of Robert de Harcourt, Bishop of Coutances (1291–1315), the King of England was moved to write to the bishop demanding that neither he nor his deputies should cite any inhabitant of Guernsey, Jersey, Sark or Alderney to appear in the ecclesiastical court in matters which pertained to the king.[9]

There are a substantial number of these cases in the records of pleas heard by the royal justices in Jersey in 1299 and 1309. An example of the uncertainties prevalent in this area is the action to enforce a deed of assignment for her dower brought by Margaret, the widow of William de Samarès, against William's heir. Margaret's case was heard by the royal justices in Jersey in 1299, but Margaret had in the meantime also taken her case to the bishop's court in Coutances. When the royal justices determined the case in her favour, Margaret was, quite naturally, willing to drop the action in the bishop's court.[10] Evidently there were aspects of this case which meant that it could come within the jurisdiction of both the secular court and the ecclesiastical court.

In the Samarès case, there does not seem to have been any objection to the jurisdiction of the bishop of Coutances. Where a party did object, the royal justices took the opportunity to assert the Plantagenet king's jurisdiction. It appears from several cases in the 1299 assizes that the principal objection of the Jersey defendants was to the financial cost and inconvenience of having to travel to the mainland for court hearings. Their complaints about being forced to plead in the bishop's court at Coutances were satisfied by an award of damages against the plaintiff responsible for this wrong. In one case, William Pagan entered this plea against Drogo de Barentin (grandson and heir of the warden of the same name), which Drogo could not deny. The royal justices determined the case by awarding William damages against Drogo, which they obligingly assessed at 60 s.[11]

The 'official' reason for the objection, however, is evident from the form of the pleadings. The injured party had to plead that the plaintiff 'dragged him' ('ipsum traxit') into Court Christian at Coutances, 'which is under the authority of the king of France', over a plea which pertained to the king, contrary to an agreement between the kings of England and France. This form of words makes plain the Plantagenet anxiety about loss of sovereignty to the French through the exercise of jurisdiction.

The attitude of the royal justices is illustrated in a plea in 1299 involving an important Jersey landholder, Jordan Norman, lord of Vinchelez, and Philip Baldwin, a priest. Philip alleged that Jordan's late predecessor, Nicholas de Vinchelez, had promised him an annual pension, possibly for having served as Nicholas's chaplain. Jordan refused to pay the pension so Philip commenced action in the court of the bishop of Coutances to enforce payment. Before the royal justices in Jersey in 1299, Jordan pleaded his objection to being 'dragged into Court Christian'. Although the dispute could well have been within the jurisdiction of the ecclesiastical court, since it apparently involved the reward of a priest for the exercise of his spiritual office, the royal justices regarded this as a matter 'which pertained to the royal court'. Philip was summoned to appear before the royal justices but did not appear. The justices thereupon ordered that all of Philip's lay fief in Jersey should be taken into the king's hand until he had made satisfaction to the king 'for contempt' and to Jordan Norman for his damages.[12] Were the royal justices especially harsh in this case because, as a priest, Philip owed obedience to the bishop of Coutances as well as to the Plantagenet king?

Notwithstanding these grievances, the potential for conflict between the secular and ecclesiastical authorities in Jersey after 1204 was not as severe as it might have been. This was due to the fact that all of the parish churches and priories were held by Norman religious houses rather than by the lay fief-holders or by English abbeys. There was no inherent conflict between the

Norman abbots and the bishop of Coutances when it came to administering these churches. In contrast, if the right of patronage of parish churches in Jersey had pertained to the lordship of a manor, as it commonly did in England, there would have been conflict between lay seigneurs, whose political allegiance lay with the Plantagenets, and the ecclesiastical authorities based in Normandy. Similarly, if English abbeys had possessed any of the parish churches or priories, the loyalties of the abbots would have been divided at times between the same powers. There might also have been more support for the transfer of ecclesiastical authority to an English diocese. The legal situation as it emerged, in fact, whereby the Norman church held uncontested ecclesiastical jurisdiction, while civil jurisdiction was vested in the king of England, was paradoxical but not unstable.

CHAPTER SIX

Law and government, 1204–1259

The Wardens: 'All the King's Men'

For most of the medieval and modern history of Jersey, the authority of the English crown was vested in two distinct offices, Warden (later Lieutenant-Governor) and Bailiff. Customarily, the Warden, the representative of the Crown, was an outsider, but the Bailiff was a Jerseyman, knowledgeable in local law and representative of local interests. The same offices existed in Guernsey, but the two islands were and are governed independently of each other as two separate bailiwicks. In the period we are examining, 1204 to 1259, these distinctions did not apply. After 1212, one royal official was responsible for all of the Channel Islands, and contemporaries might refer to them collectively as 'the King's Islands'. Nevertheless in royal mandates it was normal to name the Islands – Jersey, Guernsey, Alderney, Sark and Herm – as an acknowledgment that each island maintained its own local government.

The offices of 'Warden' and 'Bailiff' did not exist until the second half of the thirteenth century. Instead, the Plantagenet king's authority was delegated to one man. The office evolved rapidly from an essentially military role in the immediate aftermath of 1204. The king's principal representative was responsible for the conduct of all aspects of royal government – military, judicial and financial. As one would expect with a novel institution in the medieval period, there was no formal title attached to the office. The conventional form of words used by the royal chancery in letters of appointment was that the King had granted the Channel Islands 'for keeping' ('custodiendos'). From this, the office-holder might be described as 'custos'. But the same individual might also be referred to as 'ballivus', which similarly meant 'one who keeps or looks after his lord's interests'. 'Ballivus' was used in this period as a generic term for officials rather than the title of a particular office. Philip de Aubigné, whom we would regard as a Warden, styled himself 'ballivus insularum' in 1218. While the king's principal representative in the Channel Islands could be styled 'ballivus', equally his subordinates could be referred to as 'ballivi'.[1] Since the terms 'custos' and 'ballivus' taken literally both mean 'keeper, one who looks after [his lord's interests]', both could be translated in modern English as 'warden' (derived from the same French word as modern English 'guardian'). For convenience and respecting tradition, we have used the title 'Warden' to refer to the king's principal representative in the Channel Islands, but it must be borne in mind that no particular title was current before 1259.

The Wardens were appointed at the king's pleasure, and it was the king's pleasure to change them with remarkable frequency. Although there was a change of incumbent sometimes twice in a year, the office in fact circulated among a small number of royal servants. Philip de Aubigné, Geoffrey de Lucy, Richard de Gray, Henry de Trubleville and Drogo de Barentin all held it more than once. This makes sense when one considers the office of Warden of the Channel Islands in the wider context of service of the Plantagenet kings, especially in the administration of Gascony and in foreign affairs. These men held a variety of different offices and commissions during their careers, often simultaneously. Warden of the Channel Islands was just one office or duty which might be fulfilled by a member of this class of professional warriors and administrators while in the king's service.

In Chapter Three, we discussed the nexus between the influence of Peter des Roches, the Anglo-Breton aristocracy and the defence of the south coast of England with appointments to the office of Warden after 1204. This pattern continued until 1226, with the tenure of Philip de Aubigné, succeeded by his nephew and namesake, then Geoffrey de Lucy again, when coastal defence was paramount between 1224 and 1226. After the loss of Poitou in 1224, the office of Warden of the Channel Islands instead became more closely connected with the *corps* of royal servants operating between England and Gascony and generally aiding Henry III's foreign affairs, both diplomatically and militarily.

As professional royal servants, the various Wardens did not receive a salary or other reward specifically for their office in the Islands. They received grants of land in England and pensions and gifts from the king to sustain them in whatever service or services they happened to be performing anywhere in the British Isles, France or beyond from time to time. William de Bouelles, Warden for six months after the death of Henry de Trubleville in December 1239, received the land in Suffolk which the late William de Commendas had held of the king.[2] Commendas, it will be recalled, was a household knight of Henry III who had also been given the fief of Morville in Jersey (itself 'terra Normannorum') for his maintenance. The Wardens did not normally gain any personal tenurial interest in the Channel Islands. Philip de Aubigné apparently misappropriated some royal domain in Jersey for the dowry of his niece when she married Philip de Carteret. Drogo de Barentin was unusual in acquiring the fief of Rozel in hereditary tenure while he was Warden and thereby founding a dynasty of Jersey tenants-in-chief.

The office of Warden was not a full-time occupation and the Warden was not normally resident in the Channel Islands. The only regular visits would have been to take the assizes at three-yearly intervals. Otherwise Wardens visited only when their other duties and their itineraries permitted. One reason for the close connection between tenure and service in the Channel Islands and service in Brittany and Gascony was that the Channel Islands could be visited en route between England and Gascony. A letter from Philip de Aubigné to Henry III in which he describes a visit to Guernsey and Jersey to inspect the castles and thwart an anti-Plantagenet conspiracy, and begs the King to send him four or five galleys to defend the Islands, ends with the assurance that as soon as Philip has secured the castles he will return to the King.[3]

With the Warden himself an absentee, royal government must normally have been conducted by deputies. Royal mandates addressed to the Warden sometimes referred to his 'ballivi', or were even addressed directly to the 'ballivi' of Jersey and Guernsey. These were the men who were in practice going to execute the king's orders. The Warden may have appointed the deputies, no doubt a useful source of patronage for the benefit of his family and servants, but the deputies were not strictly his subordinates, in that royal mandates were not always addressed to the Warden to be delegated by him. An example is the appointment of Hugh de Saint-Philibert as Warden of Jersey for just four months in 1226. Hugh was to all intents and purposes the deputy of Geoffrey de Lucy, yet he was formally appointed as Warden ('custos') and submitted his own account to the Crown. The office of Warden was restricted to royal servants and was never offered to natives of the Islands. The exception which proves this rule is that in September 1232 Henry III had letters drafted granting custody of the Islands to Philip de Carteret and Amaury de Saint-Amand (the latter a royal familiar), but the letters were cancelled and the trusty Philip de Aubigné was reappointed instead.[4] It is possible that Philip de Carteret (de Aubigné's nephew-by-marriage) was in fact authorized to act as deputy warden ('ballivus') in Jersey at this time. As will be seen below, a decade later Philip de Carteret was named in a royal mandate in a capacity which rather resembles that of Bailiff.

There was apparently one other important office, in addition to that of Warden, which was held by the king's own men. The 'constabularius' was effectively governor of the castles of Jersey and Guernsey and commander of the garrisons. From 1232 to 1238, at least, this office was held by Gerard de Lambrusard, one of Henry III's 'alien' servants.[5]

From 'ballivus' to bailiff

In general, the 'ballivi' responsible for executing royal mandates in Jersey were Jerseymen. It was a matter of practicality that they should be resident. The effect of this was that there was a range of important offices to be held by Jersey landholders. One such office was Receiver of the Royal Revenues, which had emerged as a separate office by 1299 (see pp. 103–4, 171–2). In the thirteenth century the various offices were not all clearly distinguished, at least not with titles. An inquest jury, some decades after the event, named Jordan de la Hougue as 'vicecomes' of the Warden, Drogo de Barentin. Was this any different from a 'ballivus'? King John is said to have decreed that men should be appointed to keep the ports, but there is no record of a 'Keeper of the Ports' for Jersey or Guernsey before 1259. This does not mean that John's mandate was ignored, rather that responsibility for the security of the ports in each island was delegated to one or more 'ballivi'.

One function that must have been performed by 'ballivi' in this period was holding sessions of the royal court, in addition to the three-yearly session known as the 'assizes'. The royal court was also the manorial court for the royal domain, and the seigneurial court for tenants-in-chief, so it must have sat frequently, more frequently than the Warden could have managed. By 1300, the royal court had three principal sessions each year. The exercise of royal justice was the source of both the office of Bailiff and the institution of the Jurats. One or more of the 'ballivi' would have been delegated to preside over the royal court in place of the Warden. This was a practical arrangement since the deputy, being a local man, would have known the relevant custom, both as to procedure and substantive principles of law, whereas the absentee Warden would not. By the end of the thirteenth century, we can identify the modern office of Bailiff in a particular 'ballivus', drawn from the upper ranks of Jersey society (Philip Levesque, John de Carteret, Nicholas de Cheney) and having ultimate responsibility for the administration of justice in the royal court.[6] Perhaps a transitional stage is represented by Henry III's mandate issued in 1244 to take the assizes in Jersey, Guernsey and the other islands. This was addressed, as usual, to the Warden (then Drogo de Barentin) but also to Philip de Carteret and William de Samarès senior.[7]

The 'Constitutions of King John' and the law of Jersey

Prior to 1204 the system of law in Jersey was that which applied to all of the duchy of Normandy. The 'Coutume de Normandie' was a body of legal principles sanctioned by time, by the practice of the courts under ducal jurisdiction and by rulings of the duke with the counsel of the magnates, lay and ecclesiastical. Its coherence and uniformity were the product of firm ducal authority over a long period of time, exemplified by the regular court sessions, or assizes, held by itinerant ducal justices. This essentially oral tradition was first committed to writing around 1200.

Meanwhile, throughout the twelfth century, the law of England was developing its own uniform set of principles, the 'common law' of the royal courts. After 1204, it would have been possible for the common law of England to have been extended to apply to the Channel Islands. This did not occur, being neither practical nor desirable. To have replaced the well-known customary law of Normandy with the embryonic common law of England would have caused disruption and uncertainty amongst the Islanders. Also, the development of the common law was largely driven by the issue of particular writs from the royal chancery at Westminster, but it was so difficult for the Islanders to obtain writs that at an early date they were allowed special privileges to sue in the royal court (held in the Islands) without writ. Convergence in law with England was not desirable because King John and Henry III after him anticipated that one day Normandy would be restored to Plantagenet rule, in which case the Channel Islands would have resumed their historical status as part of the duchy of Normandy. It was therefore preferable for their legal system to remain harmonious with that of Normandy. The 'Coutume de Normandie' remained the law of Jersey, except that from 1204 the 'Coutume' came to be supplemented with any principles and procedures that became customary in the royal court of Jersey. Thus the unique customary law of Jersey evolved.

The earliest such divergence from the law of Normandy may be attributed to King John himself, in the act known as the 'Constitutions of King John'. The longer and more frequently cited version of this text, which contains detailed provisions regarding the office of Jurat and the procedure of the royal court, appears to date from the late thirteenth or fourteenth century.[8]

There is, however, a version of the 'Constitutions of King John' that may reflect accurately the terms of a document which could have been issued by John between 1204 and 1216. This is preserved as part of the return of an inquest conducted by Drogo de Barentin as Warden. By a writ dated 11 September 1248, Henry III ordered Drogo to conduct an inquest into the rents and services due from the Islanders to the Crown, and also to ascertain what laws the King's father, King John, had instituted in the Islands. Drogo was ordered to attach his seal to the record of the inquest and send it to the King, with the original mandate attached. What appears to be part of the record of this inquest, concerning Guernsey, survives in the Public Record Office as a single sheet of parchment, with the royal writ (but not Drogo's seal) duly attached.[9]

As an appendix to the Guernsey inquest, a contemporary scribe has written, on the same sheet of parchment, the heading 'Constitutiones et provisiones constitute per dominum Johannem regem postquam Normannia alienata fuit' ('Constitutions and provisions constituted by the Lord King John after Normandy was alienated'), followed by eight clauses concerning the administration of the Channel Islands (not specifically Jersey or Guernsey). This text is the earliest source for the 'Constitutions of King John' and, in our opinion, it is the only one that embodies enactments of King John without later additions. It is not the actual text of John's mandate, because it is phrased in the third person, instead of the first-person plural (the 'royal We'), and because it contains commentary on two of the 'constitutions' (to the effect that, after John's death, Philip de Aubigné had petitioned Henry III to alter them).This does not mean that this text does not accurately reflect the terms of the original document. In 1248 the reign of King John was still within living memory, and the commentary just mentioned indicates that the original measures had been introduced before the accession of Henry III. Also in favour of creation by John is the fact that, whatever his faults, the King was genuinely interested in law and administration. One imagines he would have been pleased to develop the law and institutions of Jersey and Guernsey.

All of the 'constitutions', eight in total, deal in some sense with government, but as noted in Chapter Three (see pp. 109–110), all but the first two concern the security of the Islands and the regulation of commerce and the fishing industry. These provisions addressed the situation in the aftermath of 1204, though the only ones of lasting significance were those concerning the fishing industry and *éperquerie*, which we have discussed earlier. It is the first two 'constitutions', which deal with legal procedure, that are relevant to the present discussion. Even these may have been an *ad hoc* response to the sudden rupture of the Islands from the system of justice in Normandy, but were never reversed and were enshrined as the first two articles in the fourteenth-century 'Constitutions of King John'.

The first 'constitution' recites that King John instituted twelve sworn coroners ('coronatores juratos') who were to keep the pleas of the Crown and other rights pertaining to the Crown. The duties of the 'coronatores' as first constituted by King John in Jersey and Guernsey are quite clear by analogy with the office of coroner in England, which had only been created recently, in September 1194. King John contributed to the development of the institution in England in 1200 by permitting various boroughs to elect their own coroners, which makes it even more probable that he also promoted this institution in the Channel Islands. If the office of 'coroner' was new in 1194, the duty of keeping the pleas of the Crown was not: it had hitherto formed part of the many duties of the sheriff and his deputies. Since there were pleas of the Crown, and officials whose duty it was to keep them, in Normandy as well as in England prior to 1194, the Islanders would have been quite familiar with the duties this entailed.[10]

'Pleas of the Crown' were essentially anything that infringed the King's Peace. They included all matters that are now regarded as criminal — assault, rape, abduction, murder, arson. The 'other rights' pertaining to the Crown would include matters such as treasure trove, obstruction of the highway, wreck of the sea and escheats — land, rights and revenues that should be in the king's hand because of death or other default by the tenant. The duty of the coroner was to investigate and record breaches of the peace and infringements of the Crown's rights. Hence one of his duties in England, and the one that has persisted, was to view the body of any person who had died in suspicious circumstances. Having discovered some wrongdoing, the coroner's duty was first to determine whether it constituted a breach of the King's Peace and was within the jurisdiction of the King's court, or was merely a petty offence which might be dealt with by the local court. In the Channel Islands, this might have involved the process of 'Clameur de Haro'. If the victim of some injury raised the 'Clameur de Haro', the effect was to transform the matter into a breach of the King's Peace, justiciable in the royal court. The question then arose as to whether the 'Clameur' had been conducted properly.[11] 'Keeping' the pleas especially involved the duty to keep a record of the names of parties and the circumstances of the case (in England, one of the four coroners of each shire had to be a clerk), and if necessary to impound evidence and arrest and imprison a suspected wrongdoer, and arrange for some security for his or her appearance in court before the royal justices. The culmination of the coroners' work was the presentation of all their information to the royal justices when they came to the locality to hold the royal court. The institution of coroners in Jersey was, then, merely a logical extension of a new institution operating in England which was an efficient way of ensuring that both matters of law and order and the rights of the Crown were systematically brought before the king's justices.

The second 'constitution' provides that, 'for the security of the Islands', the Warden ('ballivus'), under the supervision of the coroners, is authorized to deal with pleas of *novel disseisin*, *mort d'ancestor* and dower commenced within one year, and pleas concerning the mortgage of fiefs and encumbrance of dowry commenced at any time, without a writ. The significance of this is that these were all civil actions that could be tried in the royal court, but legal proceedings of this nature could only be initiated by the issue of a writ in the king's name. The problem that faced the Plantagenet administration in the Channel Islands, from 1206, was where such writs could be issued. They could no longer be issued in Normandy, since the Plantagenets had lost their jurisdiction there. They could be obtained from the royal chancery at Westminster, with great inconvenience and expense, but the chancery at Westminster issued writs for suits brought under the principles of the English common law, not the 'Coutume de Normandie'. So, from the point of view of King John, permitting the Islanders to commence suits without writs was a way out of this conundrum. From the point of view

'Clameur de Haro' by J. R.
Le Couteur. The complainant
raises his right hand and cries,
'Haro! Haro! Haro! À l'aide
mon prince, on me fait tort!'
An artist's impression of the
performance of this ancient
ritual as recently as 1908,
when Mr John Mollet of
Royal Crescent, St Helier,
raised the Clameur to obtain
an immediate injunction on
the felling of an oak tree.
The defendant admitted he
had wrongfully attempted to
fell the tree and was fined 60
sous, the court finding that the
'Clameur de Haro' had been
properly raised.

of the Islanders, the right to commence actions in the royal
court without writ was a generous privilege. Before 1204, they
had had to send to Caen, if not further afield, to obtain writs
to sue in the ducal court; now they were saved the trouble. Similarly the Warden of the Islands, or his deputy (soon, the Bailiff),
had jurisdiction, so proceedings did not have to await a visit
by royal justices from Normandy or, latterly, from England. In the

aftermath of 1204, there must have been many disputes and grievances over landholding in the Channel Islands, such as claims by widows whose husbands had forfeited their estates, and it was very much in the interests of both the Islanders and the Plantagenet regime that these should be resolved promptly and effectively, but still in accordance with the procedures of royal justice.

The first three types of action listed in the 'constitution' are 'possessory assizes', intended as a summary form of procedure. For instance, in a case of *mort d'ancestor*, if the jury swore that the plaintiff was the lawful heir of a third party who had died in possession of the land, then the plaintiff won the case. Determination in favour of the plaintiff meant that he or she would be awarded possession of the land in question, and the defendant would be ejected, but this would not establish which of the parties to the dispute ultimately had the better right to it. This involved a different legal procedure, commenced by a 'writ of right', which was not included in the privilege. Similarly, narrow time limits applied to the three possessory assizes; actions had to be commenced within one year from when the cause of action arose. This is quite logical considering that cases with a short history would tend to be more simple and straightforward, as the evidence would be fresh in the memory of all concerned. Nevertheless, the precedent was set for particular rules of procedure in the exercise of royal justice to apply in the Channel Islands. Soon after the end of King John's reign, in fact, the privilege of procedure without writ was greatly extended. By a mandate dated 17 February 1219 Henry III's regency council ordered that Philip de Aubigné could deal with all 'assizes' without writ, provided only that the property in dispute involved a fief of half-a-knight or less.[12]

The second 'constitution of King John' recited in 1248 requires that the 'ballivus' should exercise his jurisdiction in assizes without writ 'by the view' ('per visum') of the 'coronatores'. Considering the importance of the jurisdiction now being delegated to the Warden, this was a sound precaution. The phrase 'per visum' in royal records usually means that the person doing the viewing had a specific duty to inspect what had been done by another royal official and report back to the king as to whether the job had been done satisfactorily and whether expenditure of the king's money on it was justified. In this context, it suggests that the role of the 'coronatores' was to make a record of the pleas without writ which were determined by the 'ballivus' in the Islands and present them to the king, or in practice, to the royal justices when they next came. This would have been consistent with the recording duties which formed the basis of the coroners' role as 'keepers' of the pleas of the Crown. It would also have fulfilled the require- ment of the English common law for written record of cases determined in the royal court, since without a writ issued by the royal chancery there would be no other record of such cases. At the same time it made the 'ballivus' accountable for his exercise of this jurisdiction. Since the coroners were knowledgeable both in legal procedure and in the factual issues, it is easy to imagine that their role soon expanded from passively recording proceed- ings to advising the 'ballivus' in his determination of cases. The possible evolution from 'coronatores' to Jurats will be discussed below.

The mandate of 1219 and the first two 'constitutions' of King John deal exclusively with issues of legal procedure, as distinct from the principles of substantive law. The issue of which law should apply in Jersey, that of England or Normandy, was directly addressed by the regents of the young Henry III almost as soon as the Channel Islands were restored to Plantagenet rule. Their decision is recorded in two mandates which are of the most fundamental importance for the constitution of the Channel Islands. First, on 13 February 1218, the regency council issued a mandate in the infant king's name, addressed to the Warden, Philip de Aubigné:

> Take notice that we are advised not to institute new assizes in the Islands at present, but we wish that those assizes which were there in the time of King Henry our grandfather, King Richard our uncle and the lord King John our father should now be observed. And we have ordered for all of our said Islands by our letters patent which we send to you [that] we wish that you should cause to be observed in these same Islands the assizes which were there in the times of our predecessors.[13]

In this context, 'assize' ('assisa') had a happily ambiguous meaning. It applied to a session of a court (literally a sitting), to a type of civil procedure of the royal court (as in the 'possessory assizes' mentioned above), or to a ruling of that court. During the reign of Henry II, in the last of these senses, 'assizes' were the nearest thing to legislation – prescriptive rules promulgated by the king with the consent of his magnates, the suitors of the royal court. In respect of the royal letters of 13 February 1218, it is probably not necessary to distinguish between the different meanings of 'assize'. The significance of this is that the King undertook not to introduce new laws or innovations in the exercise of royal jurisdiction, substantive or procedural. This may have been intended as a temporary measure ('at present'), but with time it became enshrined and immutable.

The mandate of February 1218 does not mention 'custom' explicitly, although its effect was to enshrine whatever had been the substantive laws and the procedure of the royal court in Jersey before 1216 as custom. The idea of 'custom' was made explicit, however, in a further mandate one year later. In February 1219, the regency council ordered Philip de Aubigné to collect hearth-tax ('focagium') in the islands of Jersey, Guernsey, Sark and Alderney, 'according to the usage and custom of Normandy'.[14] So in the important matter of taxation, the Islanders were to be subject to the custom of Normandy.

The preservation of the customary law of the Islands was no doubt popular with the Islanders, as well as being a pragmatic arrangement. Familiar legal principles were retained, and it was convenient to be able to refer to legal authorities in Coutances or Caen for interpretation of the customary law of Normandy. Its great disadvantage was that it created for the Plantagenet kings and their deputies in the Channel Islands the problem of not actu-ally knowing what the 'law' was in any of the Islands at any given time. This embarrassment is apparent from the repeated demands of the kings and their justices for sworn testimony from the Islanders – inquests – to set out clearly and comprehensively 'the customs of the Islands'. The inquest of 1248 which gave rise to the first redaction of the 'Constitutions of King John' was but one of these, and probably not the first. Fifty years later, at the assizes held by the royal justices in 1299, there was a further attempt to per-suade the Islanders to produce a written version of their customary law, but in the end it proved too difficult: those respon-sible complained that with all the work they had to do for the assizes, it would take too much of their time.

The twelve Jurats

The institution of the twelve Jurats, as described in detail in the later version of the 'Constitutions of King John', evolved during the thirteenth century from a combination of sources. So closely is the institution of Jurat associated with the ancient liberties of Jersey and Guernsey that it is tempting to see its origins in remote antiquity, when the 'proto-jurat' may have functioned as the leader of the community of the parish. While such an origin is not impossible, there is no direct evidence for it.

The role of the institution of twelve 'coronatores jurati', as created by King John, in the history of the Jurats is ambiguous. The Jurats had in common with the coroners the duties of keeping record, but to a much greater extent, since the Jurats kept the record of all proceedings in the king's courts in the Islands. This could have evolved, however, from the duty of the 'coronatores' in Jersey to oversee the 'ballivus' in his exercise of royal jurisdiction without writ. In other respects the Jurats and coroners were quite different. There were twelve Jurats for each of Jersey and Guernsey, but the first 'constitution', apparently applicable to both Jersey and Guernsey, specifies just twelve 'coronatores jurati'. Were the twelve to be shared between the two islands? Or were there to be twelve for each? Since four coroners (three knights and a clerk) were deemed sufficient for a whole English shire in 1194, twelve should have been ample for Jersey and Guernsey together. By the end of the thirteenth century, in reverse of the development in England, the duty of keeping pleas of the Crown in the Islands had fallen to the Bailiff. The 'coronatores' had either been abolished, or the office had evolved into that of Jurat, with the original, more arduous and less prestigious duties delegated to the Bailiff.

For the further development of the institution of the Jurats, the next clue is in the mandate by the regents of the infant Henry III in February 1218, recited above. This formally established the principle that the Channel Islands would be ruled according to the laws as they stood in 1204, or more correctly, in 1216. Henceforth, there would be increasing divergence between the customs of the Channel Islands and those of Normandy, and the common law of England. From 1204, the Wardens of the Islands and the royal justices were not themselves natives of the Channel Islands; they were royal administrators familiar with the English legal system and that of Gascony. They could not therefore be expected to know the increasingly distinct and sophisticated 'custom' of each of the Islands. Twelfth-century judicial procedure already had a mechanism to meet this situation. This was a panel of knowledgeable and trustworthy men, under oath (hence they were 'jurati', a jury), who would inform the royal court of the local custom applicable in the case. In England, there was a limited future for this procedure, as customs of shires and baronies were progressively eroded by the growth of the common law. But in France, the proof of regional custom in the royal court, the Parlement at Paris, was an increasingly important area of procedure in the thirteenth century. As the diverse and semi-autonomous principalities of France were brought under royal authority, legal cases from them went on appeal to the Parlement. Here a similar procedure developed to that in England. A panel of men who were knowledgeable in the relevant custom formed a unanimous opinion under oath on the relevant principles, and delivered their verdict to the royal court. Since royal justices from the Ile-de-France had jurisdiction in Normandy from 1204 (and not just in appeals, since the king of France ruled Normandy directly), the procedure of informing them of the 'Coutume de Normandie' must have been familiar to the property-owning classes of the duchy, and hence to their relatives and neighbours in the Channel Islands.

The procedure for proving regional custom, current in both England and France, could have been an important element in the development of the institution of Jurats in the Channel Islands. The qualifications required for jurors on regional customs coincide quite closely with those of the Jurats as they emerge in the second half of the thirteenth century. They needed to be men of substance who were natives, or at least landholders in the relevant region. Being tenants made them suitors of the local courts in which the custom was current, a necessary qualification since in the absence of formal education in customary law (as opposed to canon law and civil law), knowledge gained from personal attendance at court, reinforced by the experience of fathers and others who had been suitors of the court before them, was the only way of learning the custom.

Proof of custom was not the only occasion for free men, suitors at the royal court, to become 'jurati'. A letter to Henry III, complaining about the royal favour shown to the 'infideles' who had previously abjured the Islands, was sent by a group of men of Jersey or Guernsey who identified themselves as 'the king's free and sworn men of his assize' ('liberi homines et jurati de assisa sua').[15] This description is partly explained within the letter itself, where it is stated that when Philip de Aubigné was ordered to 'hold the assizes', he ordered 'us' (the writers) to swear to uphold them. It appears therefore that these 'jurati' were the suitors of the royal court, those who held land directly of the Crown. Men of the same social status could also be 'jurati' because they were called upon to take part in an important inquest, such as that convened for the survey of the Crown's rights in Jersey in 1274. On this occasion, an inquest jury called 'the Grand Jury of the Island' consisted of twelve men. Were they the Jurats?

A particular context for 'juratus' appears repeatedly in the records of the royal court in Jersey in the thirteenth century. This is the body of men described as 'jurati de assisa'. It appears that part of the procedure for the assizes was that these suitors should attend and swear to 'hold the assize', presumably to respect and uphold the procedure and the decisions of the court. A chronological development may be observed from the few records available. In a record of assizes held by Philip de Aubigné as Warden, Philip's act is attested by seven Jersey tenants-in-chief, with no particular description or titles.[16] In the letter to Henry III just mentioned, there are no names but the suitors of the royal court describe themselves as 'jurati de assisa'. From 1254, we have a record of the royal court held by John de Gray, the deputy of the Warden. The case was said to have been heard in the presence of Philip de Carteret, William de Samarès and Henry Le Canelu (a Guernsey tenant) 'and other *jurati* of the assizes'.[17] Finally in this sequence is a record of an 'assisia' held in 1269 by Hugh de Trubleville 'ballivus insularum'. This time, the record lists thirteen men as 'juratos assisie', and shows them actually conducting the proceedings and determining the case without further reference to the 'ballivus'.[18] These cases show the emergence of the practice of the Bailiff and (twelve) Jurats holding the royal court together, which is well-attested in the record of the assizes of the itinerant royal justices held in 1299.

It probably does not pay to be too rigorous about defining the nature and duties of the Jurats before the late thirteenth century, as the institution was in the process of evolving. It is, however, informative to identify some individuals whom we might categorize as early 'Jurats'. In the record from 1254, Philip de Carteret and William de Samarès are given precedence over the other unnamed 'jurati'. The 'Grand Jury' of 1274 consisted of John de Carteret, Philip de Carteret, Nicholas Dirovaud, Henry de l'Epesse, William (le Gallichan) des Augrès, William Hastein, Jordan de la Hougue, William Lemprière, Philip Levesque, Henry Pagan, Laurence Pagan and Ralph Pagan.[19] This list of names is similar to the list of 'jurati' from 1269: William de Barentin, Reginald de Carteret, Henry de l'Epesse, Philip Fondan, Ralph le Gallichan, William Hastein, Jordan de la Hougue, William Levesque, Philip Levesque, Laurence Pagan, Ralph Pagan, William de Saint-Hilaire.[20] The total of eighteen individuals named in these two lists represents the twelve most wealthy and well established families of Jersey landholders after 1204. They or their close male kin held the office of Bailiff and no doubt every other profitable office there was to be filled. By 1309, the Crown had cause to accuse the Jurats of pretending to authority over judicial proceedings which had never been granted them by royal mandate, but to no avail. This distinctive Channel Islands institution was destined to flourish.

Royal revenues and finance

The sources of royal revenue from Jersey were the same after 1204 as they had been before. Royal policy regarding the administration of the Channel Islands was generally aimed at mollifying the Islanders, but when it came to taxation the government was as zealous as ever. The traditional Norman hearth-tax ('focagium', *fouage*) continued to be levied every three years, as we know from regular royal mandates ordering the Wardens and their 'ballivi' to collect it.

What changed was the mechanism for accounting for the Crown's finances. Before 1204, accounts of the king/duke's income and expenditure for Jersey and Guernsey had been rendered annually at the Norman Exchequer at Caen. One would expect that after 1204 their accounts would have been rendered at the English Exchequer at Westminster instead. The fact that the Channel Islands do not appear in the pipe rolls, the records of the English Exchequer, indicates that financial arrangements had changed. There must have been some sort of accounting exercise to determine the Crown's income and expenditure, and this seems to have taken place in Jersey, presumably on an annual cycle. A valuable clue comes from a document of 1254, which recites that the monks of Mont Saint-Michel had long been accustomed to receiving an annual payment of alms from the Crown's revenues of Jersey totalling 4 *l.* 10 *s. tournois per annum*. These alms were paid in three equal instalments, at Easter, at the Feast of Ss. Peter and Paul (29 June) and at Michaelmas. At each term, this payment was made 'by the hand of the "ballivus" or his delegate' in the king's castle of Jersey.[21] Since the Exchequer in England held sessions at Easter and Michaelmas, it may be that the payments to the monks of Mont Saint-Michel were rendered at the time of an Exchequer of Jersey, held at Mont Orgueil. These three terms might also correspond with the dates when the tenants of the royal domain paid their rents, replenishing the coffers in the castle treasury.

By the end of the thirteenth century, the Warden's deputy for these purposes was an official with the title of Receiver ('receptor'). The office had no doubt existed for some time before, but the first on record is William de la Hougue. William was sued by

William Godel and Denis le Fevre for wages due to them for service in the castle garrison under Nicholas de Cheney (Warden, 1297-1298). It was a point of principle in Jersey that none should be obliged to perform military service as the service due for his tenement; remuneration was expected. Before the royal justices in 1299, William acknowledged that he had wrongfully withheld the payments and he satisfied both men's claims.[22] This case provides further evidence that the Receiver disbursed funds as well as receiving them. Another example is that the prior of St Helier of the Islet asserted that, whenever the hearth-tax was levied, he was entitled to receive the amount that had been collected from his own tenants, from the hand of the Receiver.

In general terms, after 1204, all revenues received by the Crown from Jersey were applied to the cost of governing and defending the island. It seems that expenditure always exceeded income, primarily due to the costs of the rapid construction of a stone castle, and maintaining its garrison, armoury and stores, which were out of all proportion to the regular royal revenues from the island. From an early date, there are records of extra payments made to the Wardens to subsidize the military effort. In August 1225, for instance, Henry III received £100 sterling from the Knights Templar in London for the support of the Channel Islands to be delivered to Geoffrey de Lucy, then Warden.[23]

By the mid-thirteenth century things had settled down. From 1240 until 1254, when the Channel Islands were granted to the King's son, Prince Edward, the Warden held the Islands at farm. Drogo de Barentin and John de Gray in turn offered the not particularly large sums of 350 or 400 marcs of silver each year for the Islands, on the basis that they would meet the costs of administering the Islands out of their own pockets. Collection of the royal revenues and accounting for them were then left to the Warden to administer. The Crown was satisfied as long as the annual farm was paid. In the event, it was not. Drogo went chronically into arrears in his payment of the farm but was eventually 'forgiven' his debt.

The community of the parish

So far in this chapter we have examined the government of Jersey after 1204 from the top down – the King, the Wardens, Bailiffs and Jurats. Underlying the edifice of royal government, however, were institutions of local government, justice, and law and order. These remain obscure in the thirteenth century due to lack of written sources, but there can be little doubt that the principal unit of local government was the parish. The twelve parishes had a civil significance in addition to their ecclesiastical functions, and this would have changed little after 1204. The same institutions and activities of the parish in law and government probably continued comparatively unaffected by the separation from Normandy. As noted in Chapter Two (see p. 48), the three ministeria of Jersey in 1180 appear to represent groupings of four parishes. When the Crown's rights in the island were surveyed (the 'extents', the earliest being that of 1274), the enquiry was made on a parish-by-parish basis, with a jury being empanelled for each parish in turn and the written record being divided up by parishes. It was, and still is, usual to identify a parcel of land by the parish in which it is situated.

The parish also had a role in the maintenance of law and order. In cases of breach of the peace and offences which constituted pleas of the Crown (or, in ducal terms, pleas of the Sword), defendants were brought before the royal justices upon the indictment of a jury of six or twelve men from the parish where the offence occurred (the jury of presentment or 'harella'). Persons apprehended in breach of the peace could be secured in a prison maintained within the parish, or shared between particular parishes. Each parish had its 'bordarius', an officer of the Crown whose duty was to issue summonses to court, to distrain property, seizing it into the king's hand, and to perform other 'mean services' (the larger fiefs also had their own 'bordarii', who were officers of the lord).[24] This was an hereditary office, the services being due for the tenure of a certain parcel of land. Since land could descend to women and be divided between co-heirs, a parish might have several 'bordarii' at a time, even females, although one chief 'bordarius' was personally answerable for the discharge of the duties incumbent upon tenure of the land. The existence of the 'bordarii' indicates that the execution of royal justice, from summonses to enforcement of judgments, was carried out on a parish level.

These instances of the civil role of the parish all relate to royal government, and might indicate only that the parish was a construct of the royal government and did not exist except in relation to it. There is, however, further evidence for the parish as a community with its own identity. This is in the formalities for transfer of land in Jersey. It appears from various cases dealt with in the assizes of 1299 that the proper form for transfer of lawful possession of land ('livery of seisin') was a public proclamation made 'in the hearing of the parish'. The clerks of the royal court used a Latin formula for this procedure, 'in auditu parochie', whence the legal expression, 'ouïe de paroisse'. Upon a judgment of the royal court that the defendant had unlawfully dispossessed the plaintiff, the defendant was ordered to deliver seisin of the land to the plaintiff 'in auditu parochie'. Whatever the solemn pronouncements of the Bailiff or royal justices, it was only after a further ceremony had been performed in the parish that the plaintiff would have justice. Even a seizure of land into the king's hand by the 'bordarius' might be queried unless it was made by 'ouïe de paroisse'. Again, these examples relate directly to the operations of royal government, but transfer of land was also made by 'ouïe de paroisse' in the non-contentious transactions, probably the majority, which did not come within the purview of royal government. If the verdict of a jury was that land in dispute had been conveyed by 'ouïe de paroisse', the transaction was held to be binding on the parties. Unfortunately there is almost no contemporary evidence for this procedure which would indicate who constituted 'the parish' for this purpose, or the occasion for such hearings. The venue was the parish church: in a charter which confirms the dower of Felicia, widow of Nicholas de Cheney, it is stated that because the dower was constituted from land and rights situated in four different parishes, the particulars would be heard in each of the four parish churches. In another similar case it was further stated that the 'ouïe de paroisse' would occur in the relevant parish churches on a particular Sunday.[25]

This evidence of the 'ouïe de paroisse' enables us to glimpse the ordinary men, and possibly women, of Jersey, participating in the legal system of the island. It is most unlikely that transfer of land was the only type of business dealt with at meetings of 'the parish' at church on a Sunday after service. Without the work of the 'bordarii' and the juries of presentment in each parish, and the community of the parish at large, royal justice could not have functioned and there would have been a breakdown in law and order. Nevertheless, it is difficult to see how this would have been any different if Jersey had remained part of Normandy. Such institutions at the level of the parish or other local community were present, and indispensable, in both England and Normandy.

This leads to the conclusion that the area of greatest change in the institutions of the Channel Islands in the decades after 1204 was in the development of the royal court and its attendant offices of Bailiff and Jurat. The individuals who gained from this development were not the royal servants appointed as Wardens, and not the ordinary people of the parishes, but the wealthier Jersey landholders who held their estates directly of the Crown. The most important and wealthy might be appointed by the Crown as deputies of the Warden (at first 'ballivi', then in specific offices such as Bailiff, Receiver and Constable), and all gained in status and influence through their obligations as the suitors of the royal court.

16. Thomas Phillips, 'The Prospect of Mont Orgueill taken from the hill',
1690 (detail)

32. Thomas Phillips, 'A Prospect of the Bay, Towne of St Hillary, Castle of Elizabeth and Tower of St Aubin', *c.* 1690

33. Jacques Nicholas Bellin, 'Carte de L'Isle de Jersey', 1755

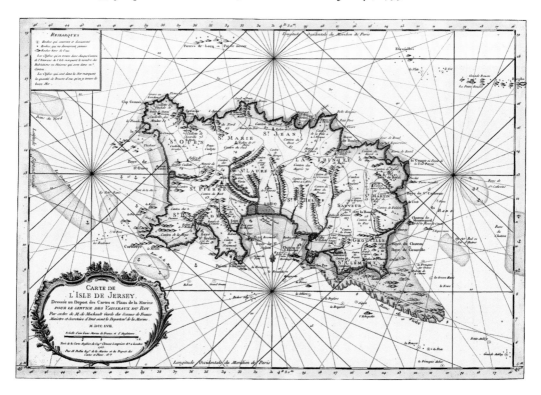

Conclusion

THE CONSEQUENCES of the loss of Normandy in 1204 have never ended: the present constitutional situation in Jersey can be traced directly back to that fateful year. It was necessary to fix a date at which to end this study, however, and we chose 1259. The loss of Normandy to the Plantagenet kings was a reality from 1204, but it was only acknowledged as such by Henry III in 1259. By the terms of the Treaty of Paris made with Louis IX in that year, Henry III secured his possession of Gascony, albeit as a vassal of the King of France. In return, Henry III formally quit to Louis IX and his heirs all the land the King of France actually possessed in the duchy of Normandy and the other former Plantagenet territories. The significance of this is evident from the fact that Henry III now ceased to use the titles 'Duke of Normandy and Count of Anjou'. The Treaty of Paris refers to 'islands' in two different contexts without making any specific reference to the Channel Islands (there were other islands off the coast of France in which the Plantagenets had interests, such as Oléron). The list of lands formally ceded to Louis IX included 'anywhere in any part of the kingdom of France or in islands (if we or our brothers or anyone in their names, should hold any)'. Since the Capetians did not possess the Channel Islands in 1259, they were not included in the surrender. The Channel Islands would, however, have been included in the second category of islands referred to in the treaty: 'islands (if any) which the king of England should hold which are of the kingdom of France'. Islands and all territories in this category, principally Gascony, were henceforth to be held by the king of England in fief, as the duke of Aquitaine, a 'peer of France', of the king of France.[1]

This must have altered the perception of the Channel Islands and their *raison d'être* as a Plantagenet territory. Since 1204, one of the most important aspects of the Channel Islands had been the fact that they were part of the duchy of Normandy. Symbolically, it was significant that King John and Henry III in turn, as 'duke of Normandy', should still possess at least a fragment of the duchy. The Islands were also a useful source of 'terra Normannorum', forfeited land with which to compensate supporters of the Plantagenets who had lost their land in France. These grants were commonly made only for a finite term, until England and Normandy should be reunited. A grant of land in Jersey in these terms was made as late as 1253.

After 1259, the Plantagenet regime must have perceived the Channel Islands more in relation to the king's status as duke of Aquitaine. The value of the Islands now lay in their role as a link between the distant northern and southern parts of the reconstituted Plantagenet empire – England and Gascony. The Islands had been involved in sea travel and commerce between these regions even before 1204, and increasingly since. This became their primary role, from the point of view of the Plantagenet regime, probably before 1259. The Plantagenet officials, the Warden and constables, were all men who were involved in the administration of Gascony. Henry de Trubleville, the Seneschal of Gascony, held the Channel Islands in fief as 'Lord of the Islands' from around 1235 until his death in December 1239.

The history of Jersey from 1204 to 1259 in terms of its administration by Plantagenet royal servants is comparatively easy to write, as this is the aspect for which the most comprehensive documentary evidence survives, in the records of royal government. Nevertheless, even the most detailed examination of the

Plantagenet administration will not yield a satisfactory answer to the question at the heart of this book. Rather, so far as the evidence permits, it is necessary to take into account the people of Jersey, their responses to the loss of Normandy and their role in the Plantagenet administration afterwards.

The Channel Islands had enormous strategic value to the Plantagenets after 1204, sufficient to warrant constant attention to, and expenditure on, their defence from French invasion. But it is unlikely that the Islands could have been successfully held by the Plantagenets for so long without the sympathy of the inhabitants. With their close proximity to Normandy, it is unlikely that the Jerseymen saw themselves as somehow becoming part of either England or Gascony after 1204. Senior royal servants, men-at-arms and merchants may have come and gone between England, Gascony and the Channel Islands, but the natives of the Islands were firmly attached to Normandy in their language and culture, in religion, commerce and law.

It may seem paradoxical, then, that the Islanders, or at least the landholders, the ones who mattered, were inclined to support the Plantagenet regime. In part, this was because the Plantagenets had the good sense to accommodate their Norman heritage. Care was taken not to force upon them changes other than those that were necessary due to the new circumstances, such as in coinage, with the substitution of the *denier tournois*, current in Capetian Normandy, for the old *denier angevin*. But if the Jersey landholders simply wanted peace and stability, they would have chosen the Capetian side, like their friends and relations on the mainland. The decisive factor was that the native Jersey landholders owed their newly elevated social, political and legal status to the separation of their community from the duchy of Normandy. Specifically, they owed everything to the disappearance of their Norman overlords, who almost all chose the Capetian allegiance and abandoned their estates in Jersey. In the aftermath of 1204, the sitting tenants of these estates quite suddenly found themselves in the privileged position of holding land directly of the Crown.

Under the Plantagenet regime after 1204 the Jerseymen had the best of all possible worlds. They were allowed to enjoy their lifestyle more or less unchanged, including contacts with the mainland. Meanwhile, the elite of the landholding class, the decision makers, enjoyed a remarkable promotion to the status of tenant-in-chief, a status they were able to enjoy with relatively light obligations to the Crown. The status of tenant-in-chief was enhanced even further by the extraordinarily self-sufficient nature of the royal court in Jersey. We can perceive this process in the early thirteenth century, mostly retrospectively from later documents, but its details remain obscure. By the end of the thirteenth century, from the commencement of action to judgment, 'royal justice' was normally administered by the Bailiff and twelve Jurats, with the aid of the suitors of the royal court, all of whom were tenants-in-chief. The Plantagenet regime in Jersey may be described as self-government under royal supervision, but the most important factor in its survival is the self-interest of the native elite whom 'self-government' had brought to power. Their determination to hold onto the power and privileges they had gained under Plantagenet rule in the aftermath of 1204 lies at the foundation of the political and constitutional status of modern Jersey.

APPENDIX ONE

The Normans and Plantagenets

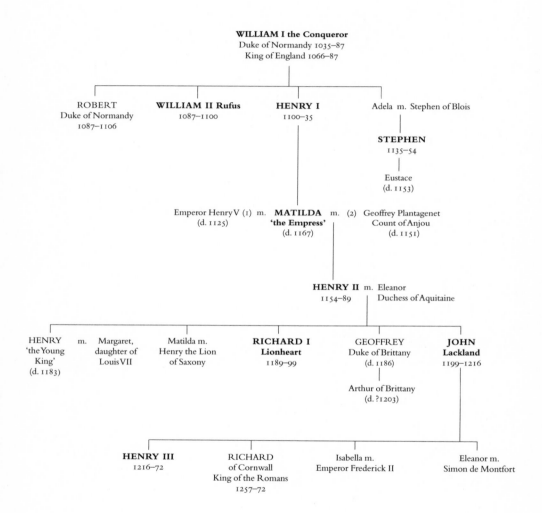

The Capetians

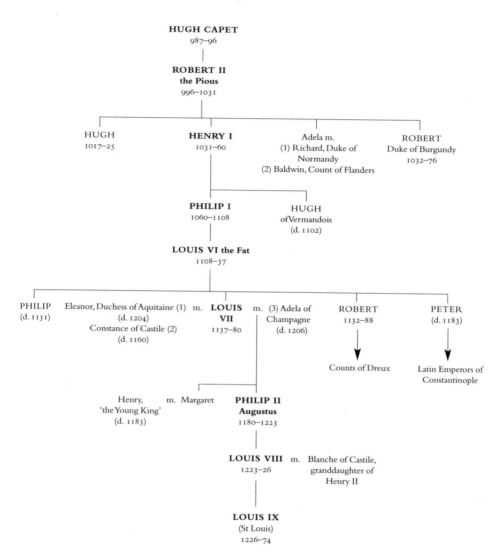

HUGH CAPET
987–96

ROBERT II
the Pious
996–1031

HUGH
1017–25

HENRY I
1031–60

Adela m.
(1) Richard, Duke of
Normandy
(2) Baldwin, Count of Flanders

ROBERT
Duke of Burgundy
1032–76

PHILIP I
1060–1108

HUGH
of Vermandois
(d. 1102)

LOUIS VI the Fat
1108–37

PHILIP
(d. 1131)

Eleanor, Duchess of Aquitaine (1)   m.   **LOUIS**   m.   (3) Adela of
(d. 1204)   **VII**   Champagne
Constance of Castile (2)   1137–80   (d. 1206)
(d. 1160)

ROBERT
1132–88

PETER
(d. 1183)

Counts of Dreux

Latin Emperors of
Constantinople

Henry,   m.   Margaret
'the Young King'
(d. 1183)

PHILIP II
Augustus
1180–1223

LOUIS VIII   m.   Blanche of Castile,
1223–26   granddaughter of
Henry II

LOUIS IX
(St Louis)
1226–74

191

Wardens of the Channel Islands, 1204–1259

CAPETIAN CONQUEST 1204–1205/6

Geoffrey de Lucy, before May 1206–August 1207 (Guernsey)

Hasculf de Subligny, before May 1206–November 1212 (Jersey)

Philip de Aubigné, August 1207–November 1212 (Guernsey)
November 1212–October 1214 (Jersey and Guernsey)
October 1214–1215 (Jersey, Guernsey and Sark)

SECOND CAPETIAN CONQUEST 1215–AUGUST 1217

Philip de Aubigné, August 1217–June 1221 (Jersey, Guernsey, Alderney and Sark)

Philip de Aubigné junior, June 1219–June 1221 *locum tenens*, June 1221–October 1224 (Jersey, Guernsey, Alderney, Sark and Herm)

Geoffrey de Lucy (Warden of the English Coast), October 1224–May 1226 (Jersey, Guernsey, Alderney, Sark and Herm)

Hugh de Saint-Philibert (assistant to Geoffrey de Lucy as Warden of the English Coast), February–May 1226 (Jersey)

Richard de Gray, May 1226–May 1227 (Jersey, Guernsey, Alderney, Sark and Herm)[1]

William de Saint-Jean, May 1227–November 1229

Richard de Gray, November 1229–July 1230

Henry de Trubleville (Seneschal of Gascony), July 1230–September 1232

Philip de Aubigné (senior), September 1232–June 1234 (departed on crusade)

Nicholas de Meules ('Molis'), June 1234–before August 1235

Drogo de Barentin, before August 1235–before May 1236

Henry de Trubleville (Seneschal of Gascony), 'Lord of the Islands', from 1236 (1234?) until death in December 1239

William de Bouelles, 'Warden of the Islands', January 1240–July 1240

Drogo de Barentin, 'Warden of the Islands', July 1240–April 1252

Richard de Gray, 'Warden of the Islands', April 1252–February 1254

Edward, Duke of Aquitaine, 'Lord of the Islands', February 1254–March 1275 (deputies included Drogo de Barentin, 1258)

Notes

CHAPTER ONE **The Plantagenet empire and the loss of Normandy**

1 *Walter Map, De Nugis Curialium: Courtiers' Trifles*, ed. and transl. M. R. James, revised by C. N. L. Brooke and R. A. B. Mynors (Oxford, 1983), p. 451.

CHAPTER TWO **Jersey before 1204**

1 Burgess (transl.), *Wace: The* Roman de Rou, p. 164, lines 2771–4
2 E. M. C. van Houts (ed. and transl.), *The* Gesta Normannorum Ducum *of William of Jumièges, Orderic Vitalis, and Robert of Torigni*, ii (Oxford, 1995), pp. 76–9
3 Burgess (transl.), *Wace: The* Roman de Rou, pp. 164–5
4 *Cartulaire*, no. 291
5 See J. N. L. Myres, 'The origin of the Jersey parishes: some suggestions', *SJBA* 22 (1977–80), 163–75, and 'The stone vaults of the Jersey churches: their historical significance', *SJBA* (1981), 85–97, and (1982), 119–200
6 See below, note 9
7 *Cartulaire*, nos 205, 206, 208
8 *Cartulaire*, no. 316
9 *Cartulaire*, no. 319
10 *Cartulaire*, no. 326
11 *Cartulaire*, no. 33
12 Edmund King, 'The Origins of the Wake Family: The Early History of the Barony of Bourne in Lincolnshire', *Northamptonshire Past and Present*, v (1975), 166–76; A. H. Ewen, 'The Fiefs of the Island of Guernsey', *SGRT*, 17 (1960–65),

173–209, at pp. 183–5; *Cartulaire*, nos 203, 209, 211
13 See Brenda Bolton, 'Esperkeria Congrorum', *SGRT*, 18 (3) (1969 for 1968), 288–96
14 Traces of other medieval buildings were found nearby, but there was scant opportunity for archaeological investigation before the sites were redeveloped. See M. B. Finlaison *et al.*, 'A medieval house at 13 and 13a Old Street, St Helier', *SJBA* (1976), 477–93, and the annual reports of the Archaeological Section of the Société Jersiaise in *SJBA*, especially the report of 1980 (*SJBA* [1981], pp. 22–3)
15 Figures supplied from *Assizes, 1309*
16 *Assizes, 1309*, p. 264
17 Paris, Bibliothèque nationale, ms français 4901, f. 22r
18 *Cartulaire*, no. 189
19 *Cartulaire*, nos 328, 329 and p. 420 n. 2; Warwick Rodwell, *Les Ecréhous, Jersey: The History and Archaeology of a Channel Islands Archipelago* (Société Jersiaise, 1996).

CHAPTER THREE **The fight for Jersey, 1204–1217**

1 We have sought to avoid over-burdening this chapter with notes. References to the mandates and other acts of King John and Henry III which are not given in the notes will be found in the editions of the early Charter Rolls, Letters Close and Letters Patent (see the list of references at p. 199).
2 *Assizes, 1309*, pp. 11–12

3 *Rot. Litt. Pat.*, p. 15

4 *Rot. Litt. Pat.*, pp. 32 and 33

5 *Recueil des actes de Philippe Auguste, roi de France*, H.-F. Delaborde *et al.* (eds), 4 vols (Paris, 1916–79), no. 803

6 *Rot. Litt. Pat.*, pp. 68 and 69

7 See Glyn S. Burgess (ed.), *Two Medieval Outlaws: Eustace the Monk and Fouke fitz Warin* (Woodbridge, 1997)

8 *Rot. Litt. Claus.*, p. 57. Eustace was not in fact the only one of his countrymen serving King John in the Channel. On 15 December 1205 the King gave permission for Ralph of Calais and his fellows in the service of Geoffrey de Lucy to come and stay in England, 'with the winnings they have taken against our enemies', as long as they remain in the king's fealty (*Rot. Litt. Pat.*, p. 57).

9 *Rot. Chart.*, p. 166

10 *Rot. Litt. Claus.*, p. 69

11 See below, note 35

12 *Chronica Rogeri de Wendover*, pp. 179–80, 221

13 *Annales monastici*, H. R. Luard (ed.) (Rolls Series, London, 1864–1869), iii, 'Annales de Dunstaplia', p. 46

14 J. Beverley Smith, 'The Treaty of Lambeth, 1217', *English Historical Review*, 94 (1979), 562–79 at p. 577

15 *Chronica Rogeri de Wendover*, pp. 59–60; Nicholas Vincent, *Peter des Roches: An Alien in English Politics, 1205–1238* (Cambridge, 1996), p. 69

16 Vincent, *Peter des Roches*, pp. 127–8. Hugh de St-Philibert, Geoffrey's deputy in English coastal defence and later in Jersey, made peace with Henry III the next day (see *Rot. Litt. Claus.*, i, 322; *Rot. Litt. Pat.*, 62).

17 *Rot. Chart.*, p. 220

18 *Patent Rolls of the reign of Henry III, AD 1216–1225* (HMSO, London, 1901), p. 108

19 See above, note 14

20 *Patent Rolls, 1216–1225*, p. 136. See p. 164.

21 *Rot. Litt. Pat.*, p. 122

22 *Rot. Litt. Claus.*, i, p. 534

23 *Royal and other Historical Letters illustrative of the Reign of Henry III*, W. W. Shirley (ed.) (Rolls Series, London, 1862–66), no. 238, pp. 286–7

24 See the report of the Archaeological Section of the Société Jersiaise in *SJBA* (1980), p. 374

25 *Cal. Inq. Misc.*, i, p. 16

26 Burgess, *Two Medieval Outlaws*, p. 21

27 *Close Rolls of the reign of Henry III, AD 1227–1231* (HMSO, London, 1902), p. 185

28 'The Account of Hugh of St Philibert, 1226', John Le Patourel (ed.), *SJBA* 15 (1949–52), 465–73 at p. 467

29 *Rot. Litt. Pat.*, p. 95

30 *Diplomatic Documents preserved in the Public Record Office, i, 1101–1272*, Pierre Chaplais (ed.) (London, 1964), p. 97

31 *Assizes, 1309*, pp. 259–60

32 *Cartulaire*, p. 28. The Warden's account for 1329 contains more details of payments received and disbursements on the quarter-days of Easter, the feast of Ss. Peter and Paul (29 June), Michaelmas and Christmas, but does not specify any location ('Accounts of John de Roches, Keeper of Jersey for the year 1329...', E. Toulmin Nicolle (ed.) *SJBA*, 7 (1912), 176–86 at pp. 177–8).

33 *Assizes, 1309*, p. 248; *Assizes, 1299*, no. 49. In fact a jury found that Simon had duly conveyed the land to William by 'ouïe de paroisse' and his case was dismissed. The records of the 1299 assizes contain other references to imprisonment, which may also have been in the castle.

34 'Accounts of John de Roches,
Keeper of Jersey for the year 1329…',
E. Toulmin Nicolle (ed.), p. 179

35 *Rot. Litt. Claus.*, p. 70

36 *The Great Roll of the Pipe, 11 John,
1209* (The Pipe Roll Society,
London), p. 66

37 *Chronica Rogeri de Wendover*, ii,
pp. 221–3. The translation given here
is from *Roger of Wendover's Flowers of
History*, 2 vols (transl. J. A. Giles)
(London, 1849, reprinted, Llanerch,
Felinfach, 1996), ii, pp. 398–9.

38 London, Public Record Office, ms
C145/2, no. 2.22a; published in *Cal.
Inq. Misc.*, i, pp. 15–18

39 *Assizes, 1309*, p. 76

40 *Mémoires pour servir de preuves à
l'histoire ecclésiastique et civile de
Bretagne*, i, H. Morice (ed.) (Paris,
1742), col. 769

41 *Rot. Litt. Claus.*, pp. 70, 92, 93, 104

42 *Calendar of Patent Rolls of the reign
of Henry III, AD 1225–32* (HMSO,
London, 1903), p. 369; *Close Rolls,
1227–1231*, pp. 409, 423

43 See the entry on Philip de Aubigné
by Professor Nicholas Vincent in the
new *Dictionary of National Biography*
(Oxford, forthcoming).

44 *Rot. Litt. Pat.*, pp. 50, 57, 62, 75

45 *Rot. Litt. Pat.*, p. 95

46 Vincent, *Peter des Roches*, pp. 160–61

47 Vincent, *Peter des Roches*, pp. 155,
161–2

48 *Patent Rolls, 1216–1225*, pp. 465, 475–6.

CHAPTER FOUR **Land and people**

1 *Assizes, 1309*, pp. 55–7; J. H. Le
Patourel, *The Medieval Administration
of the Channel Islands 1199–1399*
(Oxford, 1937) p. 57

2 *Cartulaire*, nos 189, 215; *Rot. Litt.
Claus.*, p. 181

3 *Extente, 1274*, p. 17; *Extente, 1331*, p. 37

4 *Cartulaire*, no. 3

5 *Cartulaire*, nos 151, 33

6 *Cartulaire*, no. 169

7 See *Charters of the Redvers family and
the Earldom of Devon, 1090–1217*,
Robert Bearman (ed.) (Devon and
Cornwall Record Society, Exeter,
1994)

8 *Cartulaire*, no. 170, no. 181 at p. 262,
no. 212

9 *Extente, 1274*, p. 19

10 *Cartulaire*, nos 208, 209, 211

11 The Channel Islands are fortunate in
that a catalogue of the tenements that
were forfeited and those that were
not has been published by Dr Wendy
Stevenson in 'English Rule in the
Channel Islands in a Period of
Transition 1204–1259', *SGRT*, 20
(1976–80), 234–58 at pp. 251–8

12 See Daniel Power, 'The French
interests of the Marshal earls of
Strigoil and Pembroke, 1189–1234',
Anglo-Norman Studies, 25 (2002) and
works cited there

13 *Assizes, 1309*, p. 12

14 *Rot. Chart.*, pp. 189, 192

15 *Cartulaire*, no. 325

16 *Rot. Litt. Claus.*, p. 93; *Rot. Chart.*,
p. 189; *Extente, 1274*, pp. 8 and 28

17 *Rot. Litt. Claus.*, p. 104; Stephen
D. Church, *The Household Knights
of King John* (Cambridge, 1999),
pp. 49–50

18 *Norman Exchequer Rolls*, pp. 241, 480

19 *Extente, 1274*, p. 24; *Calendar of
inquisitions post mortem* (HMSO,
London), i, no. 38; *Calendar of Liberate
Rolls, 1240–45* (HMSO, London), p. 249

20 Cartulary of the abbey of Cerisy
(Paris, Bibliothèque nationale, ms
nouv. acq. fr. 21659), pp. 420–21

21 *Rot. Chart.*, pp. 189, 192

22 *Cartulaire*, no. 340

23 See *English Episcopal Acta*, ix:
Winchester 1205–1238, Nicholas
Vincent (ed.) (Oxford, 1994),
pp. 203–6

24 *Cal. Liberate Rolls, 1226–40*, pp. 186,
242, 408, 492; *Close Rolls of the reign
of Henry III, AD 1231–34* (HMSO,
London, 1905), pp. 284 and 358;
Close Rolls, 1237–42 (HMSO,
London, 1911), p. 382; *Extente,
1274*, p. 23; *Cartulaire*, no. 340

25 A family named Buche held land in
northern Buckinghamshire in the
late twelfth century (see *Cartulary of
Missenden Abbey*, iii, J. G. Jenkins (ed.)
(London, 1962), nos 696, 673, 677,
678), but equally an 'Aimericus
Bucche' appears in May 1200 as one
of the Poitevins who were sureties
for the homage of Hugh, Count of
La Marche, to King John (see *Rot.
Chart.*)

26 *Close Rolls, 1231–1234*, p. 211.
We may see the hand of Peter des
Roches in this; around the same time
Aimery sold all his land in Little
Kington (Dorset) to the Bishop of
Winchester, as evidenced by Aimery's
own charter (*Cal. Charter Rolls, i,
1226–57* (HMSO, London, 1903),
p. 183; see *English Episcopal Acta*, ix:
Winchester, p. 21)

27 *Calendar of Charter Rolls, 1226–57*,
p. 324

28 Around 1225, Robert son of
Geoffrey de 'Escrakevilla' gave
some of his land, 'in the parish of
Heugueville situated between
Escrakevilla and the bridge of *Roca*',
to the abbey of La Luzerne,
undertaking to render the service
due from that land to 'the lord king',
that is Philip Augustus (*Cartulaire de
la Luzerne*, M. Dubosc (ed.) (Saint-
Lô, 1878), pp. 61–2).

29 *Extente, 1274*, p. 20

30 Jordan was a Jurat in 1254 (*Cartulaire*,
no. 15) and Nicholas was one of four
Islanders charged with inspecting
Richard de Gray's work on Mont
Orgueil castle (London, Public
Record Office ms E372/98 [Pipe
Roll, 1240])

31 *Extente, 1274*, p. 20; see Stevenson,
Appendix

32 *Rot. Chart.*, p. 114

33 *Recueil des Jugements de l'Echiquier
de Normandie*, Leopold Delisle (ed.)
(Paris, 1864), no. 171

34 *Extente, 1274*, p. 19.

CHAPTER FIVE **Jersey and the
Norman Church**

1 *Rot. Litt. Claus.*, p. 92
2 *Rot. Litt. Pat.*, p. 81
3 *Rot. Litt. Claus.*, p. 92; *Cartulaire*,
no. 294
4 *Assizes, 1309*, p. 63
5 J. N. L. Myres, 'The stone vaults of
the Jersey churches: their historical
significance', *SJBA* (1981), 85–97,
and (1982), 119–200
6 Burgess, *Two Medieval Outlaws*, p. 21
7 *Assizes, 1309*, p. 64
8 *Assizes, 1309*, pp. 64–5
9 *Cartulaire*, no. 6
10 *Assizes, 1299*, no. 54
11 *Assizes, 1299*, nos 6, 7, 18
12 *Assizes, 1299*, nos 87 and 233.

CHAPTER SIX **Law and government,
1204–1259**

1 For instance a letter from Hugh de
Morville, Bishop of Coutances, to
Philip de Aubigné 'and all the king's
ballivi in the Islands' (1213)
(*Cartulaire*, no. 238).
2 *Calendar of Close Rolls, 1237–42*, p. 382
3 *Diplomatic Documents preserved in the*

Public Record Office, vol. i, 1101–1272,
Pierre Chaplais (ed.) (London, 1964),
i, p. 97

4 *Patent Rolls, 1226–32*, p. 507

5 *Calendar of Patent Rolls, 1232–47*
(HMSO, London, 1906), p. 1;
*Close Rolls of the reign of Henry III,
AD 1234–37* (HMSO, London, 1908),
pp. 65, 68; *Cartulaire*, no. 97

6 See the numerous references to these
in the records of the assizes of 1299
and 1309

7 *Cal. Pat. Rolls, 1232–47*, p. 414

8 *Jersey Prison Board Case: Memorandum
prepared for the Privy Council by W. H.
Vernon and H. Sutton* (London, 1893),
Appendix, no. 2; see also *Cartulaire*,
no. 2

9 PRO C145/2, no. 2.22a; *Cal. Inq.
Misc.*, i, pp. 15–18

10 See R. F. Hunnisett, *The Medieval
Coroner* (Cambridge, 1961). In the
Islands, as throughout Normandy,
these were known before 1204 as
'pleas of the Sword', reflecting the
sovereignty of the duke (who was
not crowned but was symbolically
invested with a ceremonial sword)
rather than the king of England.

11 For further details of the case
illustrated (p. 161), see 'Clameur de
Haro!', *SJBA*, 17 (1960), 339–41

12 *Patent Rolls, 1216–25*, p. 188

13 *Rot. Litt. Claus.*, i, p. 352

14 *Rot. Litt. Claus.*, i, p. 388

15 *Royal and Other Historical Letters
Illustrative of the Reign of Henry III*,
W. W. Shirley (ed.) (Rolls Series,
London, 1862–66), no. 238, pp. 286–7

16 *Cartulaire*, no. 14

17 *Cartulaire*, no. 15

18 *Cartulaire*, no. 73

19 *Extente, 1274*, p. 8

20 *Cartulaire*, no. 73. William de Saint-
Hilaire (or St Helier) may be related
to the lords of Samarès manor. A
thirteenth 'juratus' was the prior
of St Helier of the Islet.

21 *Cartulaire*, no. 16

22 *Assizes, 1299*, nos 19 and 65

23 *Patent Rolls*, i, p. 547

24 Tenants who held their land in
bordage tenure could owe services
other than the judicial ones
mentioned, but it appears that by
1300 a particular bordage tenement
was designated as owing these
services in respect of each parish.
See *Assizes, 1309*, pp. 170–71, 291,
295.

25 *Assizes, 1299*, no. 22; *Assizes, 1309*,
p. 206.

Conclusion

1 The 1259 Treaty of Paris is published
in *English Historical Documents,
1189–1327*, H. Rothwell (ed.)
(London, 1975), pp. 376–9 (English
translation) and *Diplomatic documents
preserved in the Public Record Office,
vol. 1, 1101–1272*, Pierre Chaplais
(ed.) (London, 1964), nos 302–305.

APPENDIX TWO **Wardens of the
Channel Islands, 1204–1259**

1 From this date, all five named islands
were included in all grants of the
office of 'Warden of the [King's]
Islands'.

Notes

References cited in the notes [with abbreviations]

Calendar of Inquisitions Miscellaneous, i (HMSO, London, 1916) [*Cal. Inq. Misc.*]

Calendar of Inquisitions Miscellaneous – Chancery, preserved in the Public Record Office, i, H. C. Maxwell Lyte (ed.) (London, 1916) [*Cal. Inq. Misc.*, i]

Cartulaire de Jersey, Guernsey et les autres Iles Normandes: Recueil de documents concernant l'histoire de ces îles conservés aux Archives du Département de la Manche (Société Jersiaise, St Helier, 6 fascicules, 1918–1924) [*Cartulaire*]

Chronica Rogeri de Wendover, sive Flores Historiarum, ii, H. G. Hewlett (ed.) (Rolls Series, London, 1887) [*Chronica Rogeri de Wendover*]

Extente de l'Ile de Jersey, 1331, Edouard III (St Helier, 1876) [*Extente, 1331*]

Extente des Iles de Jersey, Guernesey, Aurigny et Serk; suivie des Inquisitions dans les Iles de Jersey et Guernesey, 1274, Edouard I (Société Jersiaise, Publication no. 2, 1877) [*Extente, 1274*]

Magni Rotuli Scaccarii Normannie, Thomas Stapleton (ed.) (London, 1840) [*Norman Exchequer Rolls*]

Rolls of the Assizes held in the Channel Islands in the second year of the reign of King Edward II, AD 1309 (Société Jersiaise, Publication no. 18, 1905) [*Assizes, 1309*]

Rotuli Chartarum in turri Londinensi asservati, Thomas Duffus Hardy (ed.) (Record Commission, London, 1837) [*Rot. Chart.*]

Rotuli Litterarum Clausarum, 1204–1224, Thomas Duffus Hardy (ed.) (Record Commission, London, 1833) [*Rot. Litt. Claus.*]

Rotuli Litterarum Patentium, 1201–1226, Thomas Duffus Hardy (ed.) (Record Commission, London, 1835) [*Rot. Litt. Pat.*]

Société Guernèsiaise Reports and Transactions [*SGRT*]

Société Jersiaise Bulletin Annuel [*SJBA*]

'Transcript of Rolls of the Assizes held in the Island of Jersey, AD 1299', John le Patourel (ed.) (Société Jersiaise, 1951, typescript) [*Assizes, 1299*]

Further reading

THE WORK OF Professor John Le Patourel forms the foundation of our study, especially *The Medieval Administration of the Channel Islands 1199–1399* (Oxford, 1937). Le Patourel's other important publications on the Channel Islands are conveniently collected in *Feudal Empires: Norman and Plantagenet*, edited by Michael Jones (London, 1984). The most relevant of these is 'Guernsey, Jersey and their environment in the Middle Ages', first published in *Société Guernèsiaise Reports and Transactions* (1974), 435–61.

John Le Patourel's pupil, Dr Wendy Stevenson, has in turn published some of the best work on the subject. Extracts from Dr Stevenson's doctoral thesis, 'England and Normandy, 1204–1259' (Leeds, 1974), appeared as two articles in the *Société Guernèsiaise Reports and Transactions*: 'England, France and the Channel Islands, 1204–1259', *SGRT*, 19 (1971–5), 569–76, and 'English Rule in the Channel Islands in a Period of Transition, 1204–1259', *SGRT*, 20 (1976–80), 234–58.

CHAPTER ONE **The Plantagenet empire and the loss of Normandy**

John Gillingham, *The Angevin Empire* (2nd ed, London, 2001) is an excellent introduction to the history of the 'Plantagenet empire' and the debates surrounding its existence. The latest French scholarship is presented with a different emphasis but similarly accessible style by Martin Aurell, *L'Empire des Plantagenêts, 1154–1224* (Paris, 2003). These supplement, but do not replace, F. M. Powicke, *The Loss of Normandy (1189–1204): Studies in the History of the Angevin Empire* (Manchester, 1913).

On Philip Augustus, see Jim Bradbury, *Philip Augustus, King of France, 1180–1223* (London, 1998) and J. W. Baldwin, *The Government of Philip Augustus: Foundations of French Royal Power in the Middle Ages* (Berkeley Ca., 1986). Of the many books on King John, the most interesting and useful in recent years is Stephen D. Church (ed.), *King John: New Interpretations* (Woodbridge, Suffolk, 1999), a collection of essays on different aspects of King John's reign.

CHAPTER TWO **Jersey before 1204**

Contemporary documents relied upon as sources for this chapter are published in the *Cartulaire* and indicated in the end notes. The documentary record is, however, fragmentary, and there is much to be derived from other sources, such as place names, archaeology, architectural history and numismatics. For place names, we are fortunate to have *Jersey Place Names: A Corpus of Jersey Toponymy* by Charles Stevens, Jean Arthur and Joan Stevens, revised by Frank Le Maistre (Société Jersiaise, 1986). The excavation reports by Warwick Rodwell, *The Fishermen's Chapel, Saint Brelade, Jersey* (Société Jersiaise, 1990) and *Les Ecrehous, Jersey: The History and Archaeology of a Channel Islands Archipelago* (Société Jersiaise, 1996), are highly relevant, and demonstrate how much more archaeological research still has to add to our understanding of the Channel Islands in the Middle Ages. See also Edmund Toulmin Nicolle, *The Town of St Helier: Its Rise and Development* (Jersey, 1931). On the history of the parish churches of Jersey, see John McCormack, *Channel Island Churches: A Study of the Medieval Churches and Chapels* (Chichester, 1986), but more cogently, two articles by J. N. L. Myres, 'The origin of the Jersey parish churches: some suggestions', *SJBA* 22 (1977–80), 163–75, and 'The stone vaults of the Jersey churches: their historical significance', *SJBA* (1981), 85–97, and (1982), 119–200. Numismatics is another valuable source: see A. L. T. McCammon, *Currencies of the Anglo-Norman Isles* (London, 1984), pp. 83–96, but the author's translations of the documentary sources should be treated with caution.

On the Western English Channel see A. G. Jamieson (ed.), *A People of the Sea: The Maritime History of the Channel Islands* (London, 1986), especially the chapters on the pre-historic era by Barry Cunliffe and the Middle Ages by Wendy Stevenson.

For the history of Normandy before 1204, see *A Companion to the Anglo-Norman World*, Christopher Harper-Bill and Elisabeth van Houts (eds), (Woodbridge, 2003). F. M. Powicke, *The Loss of Normandy (1189–1204)* (above) is also a valuable, detailed source for the administration of Normandy. On the early history of the duchy of Brittany, see the relevant volumes in the 'Histoire de Bretagne' series published by Ouest-France: A. Chédeville and H. Guillotel, *La Bretagne des saints et des rois, Ve-Xe siècle* (Rennes, 1984) and A. Chédeville and N.-Y. Tonnerre, *La Bretagne féodale, XIe-XIIIe siècle* (Rennes, 1987). A. H. Ewen, in 'The Breton Myth', *SGRT*, 21 (1981–5), 172–99, argues convincingly that the role of the Bretons in the history of the Channel Islands should not be over-estimated.

The two documents relied upon in this chapter for evidence of the ducal administration of Jersey in 1179–80 are the subject of detailed study in T. W. M. de Guerin, 'Notes on the early constitutional history of the Channel Islands: The Charter of 1179 and the *Vicomté* of Guernsey', *SJBA*, 9 (1919–22), 256–71 (with a plate of the original charter), and G. F. B. de Gruchy, 'The entries relating to Jersey in the Great Rolls of the Exchequer of Normandy of A.D. 1180', *SJBA*,

9 (1919–22), 18–44. An edition of the surviving fragments of records of the Exchequer of Normandy from 1180 to 1204, by Dr Vincent Moss, is due to be published by the Pipe Roll Society.

CHAPTER THREE **The fight for Jersey, 1204–1217**

See Wendy B. Stevenson, 'England, France and the Channel Islands, 1204–1259', *SGRT*, 19 (1971–5), 569–76. Glyn S. Burgess (ed.), *Two Medieval Outlaws: Eustace the Monk and Fouke fitz Warin* (Woodbridge, 1997) provides a detailed discussion of Eustace the Monk in fact and fiction.

In this chapter we have relied upon and cited the records of government preserved in the Public Record Office. These have been published in the series of Close Rolls and Patent Rolls by HMSO, London. For the records relating to the Channel Islands, convenient digests have been published by the Société Jersiaise: *Documents historiques relatifs aux Iles de la Manche tirés des archives conservées dans le Public Record Office, 1199–1244* (1879); *E Rotulis Litterarum Clausarum Excerpta ad Insulas Normanniae Spectantia, 1205–1327*, F. H. Barreau and H.-M. Godfray (eds), (Publication no. 9, part 1, 1891), and *Documents relatifs aux Iles de la Manche tirés aux rôles des lettres closes conservées au PRO à Londres, 1205–1327*, W. Nicolle (ed.), (Publication no. 9, part 2, 1893). Similarly many of the important records and their sources are collected in *Mont Orgueil Castle: A Report on the Archives*, Philip Dixon, Michael Jones and Christopher Phillpotts (eds), (Nottingham, 1998).

The classic study of Mont Orgueil is Edmund Toulmin Nicolle, *Mont Orgueil Castle: Its History and Description* (Jersey, 1921). 'Mont Orgueil', in *Current Archaeology*, no. 183, vol. XVI (3) (December 2002), 98–106, is a useful summary of recent debates on the history and future of the castle.

CHAPTER FOUR **Land and people**

G. F. B de Gruchy, *Medieval Land Tenures in Jersey* (Jersey, 1957) is an excellent account of the structure of land tenure in medieval Jersey, but is not restricted to the thirteenth century. Jersey lacks a published study to compare with A. H. Ewen, 'The Fiefs of the Island of Guernsey', *SGRT* 17 (1960–65), 173–209, which is nevertheless interesting for evidence for some families holding land in Jersey also. P. Bisson, 'The fief and seigneurs of Samarès in the middle ages', *SJBA* 24 (1985–88), 339–53, is an isolated example of the type of genealogical study that one could wish for on other Jersey families. We have relied upon the records of government in the Public Record Office (see Chapter Three above) for evidence of awards and forfeitures of land in Jersey.

Further reading

CHAPTER FIVE **Jersey and the Norman Church**

From the point of view of the Plantagenet administration, all the possessions of the Norman monasteries in Jersey were 'alien priories'. The subject of the alien priories in England would reward further research, and as regards the Channel Islands very little has been written at all. A recommended introduction is Donald Matthew, *The Norman Monasteries and their English Possessions* (Oxford, 1962). We are persuaded by the arguments of J. N. L. Myres on the development of the parish churches of Jersey in 'The stone vaults of the Jersey churches: their historical significance', *SJBA* (1981), 85–97, and (1982), 119–200.

CHAPTER SIX **Law and government, 1204–1259**

John Le Patourel, *The Medieval Administration of the Channel Islands 1199–1399* (Oxford, 1937) remains the essential starting point for this enquiry, being based on meticulous research into the manuscript sources, especially those extant in the Public Record Office in London. One of the most important classes, as Le Patourel testifies, is that of the records of the assizes held by the royal justices-in-eyre in 1299 and 1309. The 1309 eyre has been published as *Rolls of the Assizes held in the Channel Islands in the second year of the reign of King Edward II, AD 1309* (Société Jersiaise, Publication no. 18, 1905). The 1299 eyre has not been published, but the Société Jersiaise possesses a typescript edition, prepared by John Le Patourel. Some of Le Patourel's conclusions are summarized in 'The Law of the Channel Islands, 1. The origins of the Channel Islands legal system', *The Solicitor Quarterly*, 1 (1962), 198–210. See also Julien Havet, 'Les Cours Royales des Iles Normandes', *Bibliothèque de l'Ecole des Chartes*, 38 (1877), 49–96, 275–332; 39 (1878), 5–80, 199–254, and H.-M. Godfray, 'L'origine des jurés-justiciers dans les iles de la Manche', *SJBA*, 3 (1890–96), 173–90.

Conclusion

See Malcolm Vale, *The Origins of the Hundred Years War: The Angevin Legacy 1250–1340* (Oxford, 1996).

List of illustrations

Text illustrations

Plates

Index

Numbers in *italics* refer to illustrations